THE
INDISPENSABLE
GUIDE
to practically
EVERYTHING

Prayer

THE
INDISPENSABLE
GUIDE
to practically
EVERYTHING

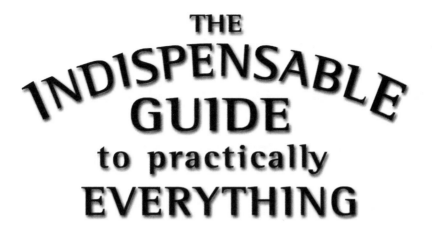

Prayer

MARCIA FORD

Guideposts
New York, New York

The Indispensable Guide to Practically Everything: Prayer

ISBN: 978-0-8249-4775-0

Published by Guideposts
16 East 34th Street
New York, New York 10016
www.Guideposts.com

Distributed by Ideals Publications, a division of Guideposts
2636 Elm Hill Pike, Suite 120
Nashville, Tennessee 37214

Guideposts and *Ideals* are registered trademarks of Guideposts.

Acknowledgments
Every attempt has been made to credit the sources of copyrighted material used in this book. If any such acknowledgment has been inadvertently omitted or miscredited, receipt of such information would be appreciated.

Scripture quotations marked CEV are from the Contemporary English Version, copyright © 1995 by the American Bible Society. Used by permission.

Scripture quotations marked HCSB are from the Holman Christian Standard Bible®, copyright © 1999, 2000, 2002, 2003 by Holman Bible Publishers. Used by permission. Holman Christian Standard Bible®, Holman CSB®, and HCSB® are federally registered trademarks of Holman Bible Publishers.

Scripture quotations marked MSG are from *The Message*. Copyright © 1993, 1994, 1995, 1996, 2000, 2001, 2002. Used by permission of NavPress Publishing Group.

Scripture quotations marked NASB are from the New American Standard Bible®, copyright © 1960, 1962, 1963, 1968, 1971, 1973, 1975, 1977, 1995 by The Lockman Foundation. Used by permission.

Scripture quotations marked NIV are from the Holy Bible, New International Version®. Copyright © 1973, 1978, 1984, International Bible Society. Used by permission of Zondervan Publishing House. All rights reserved.

Scripture quotations marked NKJV are taken from the New King James Version. Copyright © 1982 by Thomas Nelson, Inc. Used by permission. All rights reserved.

Scripture quotations marked NLT are from the *Holy Bible*, New Living Translation, copyright © 1996, 2004. Used by permission of Tyndale House Publishers, Inc., Wheaton, IL 60189. All rights reserved.

Library of Congress Cataloging-in-Publication Data

Ford, Marcia.
  Prayer / Marcia Ford.
    p. cm. – (The indispensable guide to practically everything)
  ISBN 978-0-8249-4775-0
  1. Prayer–Christianity. I. Title.
  BV210.3.F66 2010
  248.3'2–dc22
                          2009016295

Editor: Lila Empson
Cover and interior design: Whisner Design Group
Typesetting: Educational Publishing Concepts

Printed and bound in the United States of America

10 9 8 7 6 5 4 3 2 1

Prayer moves the hand which moves the world.

J. A. Wallace

Contents

Practical Matters of Prayer 61

The Lord's Prayer 87

Great Prayers of History 113

Praying in the Middle of Life for You and Others....

More things are wrought by prayer
than this world dreams of.

Alfred, Lord Tennyson

Introduction

Prayer is the vital breath of the Christian; not the thing that makes him alive, but the evidence that he is alive.

Oswald Chambers

If U.S. pollsters are to be believed, Americans are a praying people. Surveys by secular and religious polling organizations routinely report that as many as 90 percent of the nation's adults pray regularly—and half of those surveyed say they pray more than once a day. In one sense, that's an astonishing percentage; with America's melting-pot population, it's nothing short of amazing that so many people share a commitment to a single spiritual practice. And yet, in another sense, it shouldn't be surprising at all.

Prayer has undergirded this nation from its very inception, and the tradition of praying has been handed down generationally for more than

If two of you on earth agree about any matter that you pray for, it will be done for you by My Father in heaven.

Matthew 18:19 HCSB

three hundred years, with each generation—as well as each denomination, congregation, and individual—bringing its own personality and flavor to the practice.

But while Americans are particularly prayerful, Christians throughout the world also post respectful numbers in similar polls. Prayer, it seems, is inextricably woven into the multicultural fabric of Christianity.

Regardless of the passage of time, the range of locations, and the diversity of the people, down through the centuries the nature of Christian prayer has remained the same: it is a personal conversation with a personal God. Even so, prayer encompasses so many dimensions that it is a practice at once simple and complex, and people approach prayer with an abundance of questions:

- Does God really hear my prayers?

- What if my prayers aren't answered?

- Is there a right way to pray?

- How can I hear God's voice?

Christians have been asking those and other questions about prayer for two millennia, indicating the need for each generation to plumb the depths of prayer and discover for itself the meaning behind the practice. As for the questions that remain unanswered, believers have long recognized this truth: "Now we see in a mirror dimly, but then face to face; now I know in part, but then I will know fully just as I also have been fully known" (1 Corinthians 13:12 NASB).

> You'll take delight in God, the Mighty One, and look to him joyfully, boldly. You'll pray to him and he'll listen.
>
> Job 22:26–27 MSG

**Faith sees the invisible, believes the unbelievable,
and receives the impossible.**

Corrie ten Boom

Call to Me, and I will answer you,
and show you great and mighty things,
which you do not know.

Jeremiah 33:3 NKJV

If you remain in Me and My words
remain in you, ask whatever you
want and it will be done for you.

John 15:7 HCSB

Prayer 101

**Discover the basics of having a conversation with God.
Here you'll find what you need to know to start—
or jump-start—a life of prayer.**

Contents

If you have faith when you pray,
you will be given whatever you ask for.

Matthew 21:22 CEV

What Is Prayer?

Like the fictional archaeologist Indiana Jones, men and women since the dawn of time have misunderstood prayer: "Jones, do you realize what the Ark is? It's a transmitter. It's a radio for speaking to God," said Dr. Rene Belloq to Indiana Jones in *Raiders of the Lost Ark*.

People assume God will hear them better if they speak louder, shout from a mountaintop, utter the right words, or assume a certain posture. Those on earth need no transmitter to reach the ear of almighty God. They have forgotten what prayer is.

✳

Conversation with God

Prayer is having a conversation with God. Where do you have your best conversations? In the car on a long trip? On a long-distance phone call? In a diner over coffee? Snuggled up by the fire?

You remember these conversations because you and your companion were both relaxed and eager to hear what each other had to say. No agendas. Just genuine interest.

Conversation is dialogue, not a monologue. Both people want to speak and be heard. Both people draw joy from the interaction. The same is true of your conversations with God.

> Seek the LORD while He may be found, call upon Him while He is near.
>
> Isaiah 55:6 NKJV
>
> Keep on asking, and you will receive what you ask for. Keep on seeking, and you will find. Keep on knocking, and the door will be opened to you.
>
> Matthew 7:7 NLT

He Hears You

God created you for a relationship with Him. Like a friend who hasn't heard from you in a long time, God longs to chat with you. He is waiting. He is your friend!

There is no number to dial or button to push. Just speak aloud in your car or kitchen. Think your prayers at your favorite coffee shop. Share your joys and struggles. Unload your disappointments. He is listening.

Listen to Him

Have you ever had a conversation where squeezing a word into the conversation was as hard as pushing a watermelon through a keyhole? When you converse with God, allow him to comment on what he's heard. Ask him questions, and then listen for an answer. God responds to our prayers in many ways. Chapters 3-6 of this book are devoted to listening to God because it is so essential to a vibrant prayer life.

Final Thoughts

A Southern preacher from another generation once said, "God gave me two ears and one mouth so I would listen twice as much as I talk." He was echoing advice offered by the author of Ecclesiastes: "Don't be too quick to tell God what you think he wants to hear. God's in charge, not you—the less you speak, the better" (Ecclesiastes 5:2 MSG). Don't forget the second part of conversation: listening.

Myth Buster

It's a myth that God hears you better when you pray using formal language like *thee* and *thou*. God may be the King of kings, but there is no book of protocol to follow. He is also your Father (Romans 8:15). Written prayers can be helpful. They can keep you from distraction and order your thoughts. However, never mistake "organized" for "formal." Your Father will always welcome you into his lap for a chat.

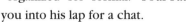

Are There Any Prerequisites for Prayer?

The parlor was the largest room in houses designed during the nineteenth century. Friends and family would spend time on Sunday afternoons visiting with other friends and family. They would dress in their Sunday finery, sit regally in the parlor, and discuss the issues of the day.

Is prayer like visiting in God's parlor? Does he expect you to meet him somewhere special? What posture are you supposed to assume? Are there special words or phrases you need to use?

Where Should You Pray?

Question: Where are you supposed to pray? Answer: You must go where God is. Psalm 139 shows God at the altitude of mountaintops and jet streams. He is also as low as valleys and ocean floors. He is where you are now. He is where you are going. God is everywhere at all times. Theologians call this character quality *omnipresence*. Since God is *everywhere*, you can pray to him *anywhere*.

> Pray constantly.
>
> 1 Thessalonians 5:17 HCSB
>
> The LORD has heard my cry for mercy; the LORD accepts my prayer.
>
> Psalm 6:9 NIV

Question: What is the correct posture for prayer? Answer: You must turn toward God. Throughout the Old and the New Testaments, men and women prayed in many different postures. They knelt in humility and reverence. Sometimes, in their anguish, they stretched out flat on their faces. They prayed with battle armor and spears at the ready. They prayed as they worked as slaves in Egypt during their captivity. Years later, after another exile from their homes, they prayed while they rebuilt the wall of Jerusalem. Throughout the ages, God's praying people had one thing in common—they had turned their hearts toward God in prayer. God is looking for the position of your heart, not the posture of your body.

How Should You Pray?

Question: What are the correct words for prayer? Answer: You must use a language God understands. Many people use a precise tone of voice and eloquent, scripted words. They make it seem that words spoken in prayer come only from a book of special phrases and words. No such book exists. As a matter of fact, even when you do not have words, you can still pray. "In the same way the Spirit also helps our weakness; for we do not know how to pray as we should, but the Spirit Himself intercedes for us with groanings too deep for words" (Romans 8:26 NASB). God listens to your heart, not just to your mouth.

Final Thoughts

There are no prerequisites for prayer. You are God's precious child. He is never too busy for you to burst into the room, hop into his lap, and open the floodgates of your heart. You are important to him. "Let us therefore come boldly to the throne of grace, that we may obtain mercy and find grace to help in time of need" (Hebrews 4:16 NKJV).

Something to Ponder

Of all the postures of prayer illustrated in the Bible, God's people never prayed sitting down. Is it wrong to pray while seated? Of course not. Remember, God is looking for the position of your heart. However, this observation can be instructive. It appears that God wants you to be active in your prayers. Even while seated, may you never become passive.

God Talks to You

Busy signals. *"Please leave a message after the tone."* *"The number you have called has been changed."* Jeremiah 33:3 is often called God's phone number: "Call to Me, and I will answer you, and show you great and mighty things, which you do not know" (NKJV). God spoke these words to his people through the prophet Jeremiah.

These words are also a promise. When you call out to God, you will never hear silence or be placed on hold. God longs to hear your prayers and respond. God is part of the dialogue of prayer through his still, small voice and the Bible.

☧

Listen for God's Voice

God's voice is hard to hear. God worked through Elijah to demonstrate his power to King Ahab, Queen Jezebel, and their entire kingdom. Jezebel became enraged and threatened Elijah's life. Despite God's amazing pyrotechnics show the day before, the prophet fled in fear. He cowered in a cave, awaiting more marching orders. As you read 1 Kings 19, you can almost see Elijah turning his head and pointing one ear toward God. The winds blew, an earthquake erupted, and fire swept over the mountain, but Elijah didn't hear God amid the fireworks. Suddenly, the Bible tells us, Elijah heard a still, small voice. A whisper.

O Lord, answer me! Answer me so these people will know that you, O Lord, are God and that you have brought them back to yourself.

1 Kings 18:37 NLT

"If you'll hold on to me for dear life," says God, "I'll get you out of any trouble. I'll give you the best of care if you'll only get to know and trust me. Call me and I'll answer, be at your side in bad times; I'll rescue you, then throw you a party. I'll give you a long life, give you a long drink of salvation!"

Psalm 91:14–16 MSG

The culture fills every second with fireworks of its own. Three hundred television channels compete with Internet videos. Satellite radio wars with the iPod. Your senses can easily be overwhelmed and stressed. Just as suddenly, just as quietly, God can speak to you. Are you turning your head and bending your ear toward his voice?

Here are a few ways to listen for the voice of God in a noisy world:

- Set aside a special chair and lamp in your home. Spend the first fifteen minutes of each day in prayer. Allow the chair to become a special meeting place for listening to God.

- Use your car as a sanctuary. Drive for a while with the radio and cell phone turned off. Or, after driving to a destination, sit quietly in your car for a few minutes before going inside.

- Make your hectic morning routine meaningful. Write prayer requests on the shower wall with children's bathroom markers. Pray and listen during bath time.

- Don't fall asleep with the television on. Instead, spend a few minutes praying and listening before fluffing your pillow.

Search the Bible

As hard as God's voice is to hear, it's even harder to make sure you heard it right. Compare what you've heard in your conscience to what God says in the Bible. This is not a display of doubt; it's a noble pursuit.

The apostle Paul and his friend Silas visited the city of Berea in Greece. They were impressed. The Bereans listened like anxious students hanging on every word of their professor, but when the teaching was over, they "searched the Scriptures daily to find out whether these things were so" (Acts 17:11 NKJV).

Don't take what you hear at face value. Take a cue from the Bereans and search out the Scriptures for confirmation. How large is your decision? How deep is your crisis? How wonderful is your possibility? Depend on the Scriptures in direct proportion.

Hearing God's Voice

In addition to listening for God's voice when you pray, you should also look for God's message to you when you read the Bible. Throughout history, Christians have tried a number of creative—but dangerous—ways to find God's message. Some have approached the Bible with eyes closed, opening the book to a random page, pointing a finger at a passage, then opening their eyes to see what God would say. Equally dangerous, some have chosen a series of numbers like a telephone number. For 123-555-1212, they've opened the Bible to page 123, counted the lines to find number 555, then read the next 1,212 characters.

> When you call, the LORD will answer; when you cry out, He will say: Here I am.
>
> Isaiah 58:9 HCSB

Instead of hunt-and-peck spirituality, seek the whole counsel of the Bible. Any less is like assuming you've seen a movie just by watching the trailer.

A topical Bible puts all the verses addressing a subject at your fingertips. Editors arrange verses by issue or thought. Look up the subjects in the same way you would use an encyclopedia. Under each division, you'll find the addresses to the Scriptures that meet your needs.

For example, if you're praying about a new job, look up words such as *work, talent, labor,* and *prosperity.* Write down the references in your journal, and then look up each one, listening for direction.

Points to Remember

A game called "Word Scramble" appears in hundreds of newspapers worldwide. Readers work hard to figure out anagrams—rearranging the letters in one word to form another. One of the anagrams that can be spelled from the word *listen* is *silent.* Will you rearrange your life in small ways to hear God's voice more clearly?

25

Myth Buster

Some say that God used burning bushes, talking donkeys, and angels to deliver his messages in the Bible but that he doesn't do anything like that anymore. Every year, Christians worldwide report hundreds of fascinating encounters with God. Your job is to have your eyes, ears, and heart wide open. Don't be like Jim Carrey's character in the movie *Bruce Almighty*. He prayed for a sign, and God sent him a truckful he didn't see.

Something to Ponder

God, please rescue me!" a man prayed as he watched the lake flood over its banks. He waited on God's answer. The mayor ordered evacuation over television, but the man waited on God's answer. Two men came by in a canoe offering a ride, but he waited on God's answer. He crawled up on the roof. A helicopter lowered a ladder, but he waited for God's answer. God talks to you. Are you listening? Hearing God requires an understanding of the many ways he responds to people. The answer to your prayer may come in unexpected ways. By remaining spiritually alert, you'll be better able to recognize the answer when it comes.

What God Says When God Talks to You

A politician gives a speech that lasts thirty minutes. The pundits spend hours—sometimes days—telling you what the politician meant. A speaker from a foreign country teaches a class. Phrase by phrase, the interpreter standing next to her translates the concepts and words into your language. The God of the universe whispers to your heart. The Bible's text is ancient, and you must work, at times, to understand its meaning. How do you know what God is saying? How do you differentiate between his voice and the voice of the Devil, the Enemy of our souls?

You Know His Voice

A baby knows the voice of his mother. Just a word can soothe a cry. A toddler can tell the difference among all the vehicles that come down his street. When his father is nearing home, the toddler moves to the door. In the same way, you know the voice of your God.

> The wisdom that comes from above leads us to be pure, friendly, gentle, sensible, kind, helpful, genuine, and sincere.
>
> James 3:17 CEV
>
> All Scripture is inspired by God and profitable for teaching, for reproof, for correction, for training in righteousness.
>
> 2 Timothy 3:16 NASB

Jesus was teaching a crowd with many religious leaders looking on. He compared himself to a shepherd and said, "The sheep follow [the shepherd] because they recognize his voice. They will never follow a stranger; instead they will run away from him, because they don't recognize the voice of strangers" (John 10:4–5 HCSB).

Take comfort in this knowledge, but be sure to take the time to distinguish between all the voices you hear in a given day. God's voice has many distinct qualities.

The Qualities of God's Voice

You know the voice of Don LaFontaine (1940–2008). He became known as "The Voice of God." The voice-over actor recorded thousands of movie trailers. He is famous for the phrase, "In a world where . . ." His "thunder throat" had many distinctive qualities. God's voice has many as well. His voice has richness and tones that set his voice apart.

James reminded us that when God speaks, he will do so with kindness and gentleness. God's wisdom comes to help and to build up. The tone of voice God uses with his children points toward peace.

The apostle Paul, in his last letter to his apprentice Timothy, summarized the roles of the Bible in your life. When God speaks in prayer, his voice will carry the same roles. God desires to teach you like a parent teaching a child to walk. He will reprove or reprimand you like a parent pulling a child back from touching a hot stove. He will correct you like a coach working on the fundamentals of a sport. He will also train you in small increments like a dance instructor.

The tone of God's voice will sound more like Mr. Miyagi, the long-suffering sensei from *The Karate Kid* than Foley, the rigid drill sergeant from *An Officer and a Gentleman*.

Recognizing the Voice of Your Enemy

Many voice-over artists have tried to imitate LaFontaine. In the same way, the Devil tries to imitate God's voice to fulfill his ultimate directive—to deceive you. He hissed his way into Eve's heart and pulled her from God's instructions in the garden of Eden. He tried to outwit Jesus after he fasted for forty days before launching his earthly ministry. Later, Jesus would tell a large group of followers that the Devil "was a murderer from the beginning, not holding to the truth, for there is no truth in him. When he lies, he speaks his native language, for he is a liar and the father of lies" (John 8:44 NIV). The Devil is also called the accuser (Revelation 12:10).

When you hear a voice, listen for half-truths, twisted words, and accusation. The Enemy wants "to steal, and to kill, and to destroy" (John 10:10 NKJV). God seeks to heal the brokenhearted and bind up their wounds (Psalm 147:3).

The Content of God's Communication

Two famous songs summarize what God will say to you. The children's song "Jesus Loves Me, This I Know" is profound in its simplicity. God loves you. The Bible is often called God's Love Letter. The most famous verse in the Bible—John 3:16—is one of dozens outlining how much God loves you. God loves you with an everlasting love.

> Come, let us bow down in worship, let us kneel before the LORD our Maker; for he is our God and we are the people of his pasture, the flock under his care. Today, if you hear his voice, do not harden your hearts.
>
> Psalm 95:6–8 NIV

The world's most famous hymn, "Amazing Grace," reminds us that God's messages will be full of grace. Grace is not escaping punishment; it is receiving a reward when you should be receiving punishment. Jesus sacrificed his life on your behalf to cover your sin so that you might go to heaven.

When you hear a voice, listen for messages filled with love and grace and discard the others. Know the differences between God's voice and that of the Devil.

29

Characteristics of the Voice of God Contrasted with the Voice of the Devil

Voice of God	Voice of the Devil
Correction	Accusation
Reproof	Shame
Pure	Twisting of the truth
Peaceful	Murderous
Gentle	Destructive
Honest	Deceptive
Fair	Self-centered
Teaching	Haughty
Righteous	Slippery

Final Thoughts

When listening for God's voice, remember these truths:

- Jesus was crushed. He will not crush you.

- Jesus was bruised. He will not bruise you.

- Jesus was mocked. He will not mock you.

- Jesus was spat upon. He will not spit on you.

- Jesus was abandoned. He will not walk away from you.

God's voice will never speak destructive, hurtful, derisive, degrading, or forsaking words to you.

How God Talks to You

Same room. Same people. Different emotions. When they arrested Jesus, the disciples retreated to the room where they had shared the Passover meal. They locked the door and wondered when guards would kick down the door and drag them away. The resurrection changed their outlook. Jesus gave some instructions and reminded them of his promise. Then Jesus ascended to heaven. They returned to the same room without fear, and they waited for the promise like eight-year-olds in late December. How does God talk to you? Through the fulfillment of that promise to the disciples—and you. The fulfillment of that promise enables and empowers your prayers.

✳

During the Passover meal with his disciples—the Last Supper—Jesus saw twelve distressed faces. He comforted them with many truths, including his promise to send the Helper. This Holy Spirit was a new concept. Jesus described the Spirit as full of truth, living in you, and staying with you no matter what.

The Holy Spirit Helps You in Your Weakness

The Holy Spirit isn't Alfred to your Batman. He is more like a battlefield medic always nearby with words of comfort and plenty of bandages.

Derek Redmond was expected to medal in the 400 meters during the 1992 Olympics, but a torn hamstring crashed him to the track with 70 meters to go. He stood and limped forward, determined to finish.

> I will ask the Father, and He will give you another Counselor to be with you forever. He is the Spirit of truth. The world is unable to receive Him because it doesn't see Him or know Him. But you do know Him, because He remains with you and will be in you.
>
> John 14:16–17 HCSB
>
> Ask me, and I will do whatever you ask. This way the Son will bring honor to the Father. I will do whatever you ask me to do.
>
> John 14:13–14 CEV

His father burst past heavy security to wrap his arm around his son. He supported his weak side all the way across the finish line.

When you pray, the Holy Spirit is like Jim Redmond—he supports you where you're weak and comforts you where you hurt.

The Holy Spirit Helps You Understand the Mind of God

When you bring your questions to God, you hope for answers. The Helper is with you and in you to help you hear and understand God. The apostle Paul described the Spirit's mission statement. He is "the spirit of wisdom and revelation in the knowledge of Him" (Ephesians 1:17 NKJV).

God talks to you in prayer through the Holy Spirit. The Spirit helps the lightbulb of comprehension glow brightly above your head.

Something to Ponder

Bill Bright (1921-2003), the founder of Campus Crusade for Christ, always spoke of the Holy Spirit as a friend: "He makes me glad. He fills my heart with joy. He inspires me with marvelous ideas. He energizes me. He surprises and blesses me daily. He listens when I need help. He has incredible wisdom and insight. When He speaks, it is as if a light goes on in my head and heart."

Check Your Understanding

- **Is the Holy Spirit equal to God?**

The Holy Spirit is God. Orthodox Christian belief holds that God is one God in three Persons—Father, Son, and Holy Spirit. The Holy Spirit is the third part of the Trinity. He is described through the Bible with the same attributes as God. The Spirit is eternal, omnipotent, omniscient, omnipresent, and was part of creating the universe.

When God Talks to You

When the night started, Samuel must have wanted a cup of warm milk and an extra blanket. His eyes had barely drooped when he heard his name. Like a good apprentice, he reported for duty to his mentor, Eli. But the aging priest hadn't called him. Samuel returned to bed only to hear two more summons. Eli figured it out and sent Samuel back to bed with instructions: if you hear your name again, it's God calling. God did call his name. Samuel responded, "Speak, for Your servant hears" (1 Samuel 3:10 NKJV). When God calls your name, how do you respond?

✳

Are You Listening?

When Eli sent Samuel back to bed to listen for the Lord, he must have heard every creak and every puff of wind. His ears were alive with anticipation. Are yours?

Eugene Peterson, pastor and creator of *The Message* Bible paraphrase, said, "We're in a hurry and not used to listening. We're trained to use our minds to get information and complete assignments; but the God revealed to us in Jesus and our Scriptures is infinitely personal and relational. Unless we take the time to be quiet, in a listening way, in the presence of God, we never get to know Him."

Train your ears to pick out the voice of God from the surface clutter of daily life.

> While [Peter] was still speaking, a bright cloud overshadowed them, and behold, a voice out of the cloud said, "This is My beloved Son, with whom I am well-pleased; listen to Him!"
>
> Matthew 17:5 NASB

> The LORD is a great God and a great King above all gods, in whose hand are the depths of the earth, the peaks of the mountains are His also. The sea is His, for it was He who made it, and His hands formed the dry land.
>
> Psalm 95:3–5 NASB

Are You Responding?

When God called Samuel, he must have popped out of bed like a husband nudged by his expecting wife to take her to the hospital.

Do you respond like Samuel? Do you spring into action with anticipation and eagerness like a young groom pursuing his bride? Do you respond like Pharaoh? Moses approached him seven times and said, "Thus says the Lord God of Israel . . ." Each time, Pharaoh turned a deaf ear. Do you respond like a cautious business owner with words like, "We need to study several alternatives to determine the best course of action"?

Decide today to grow in how you respond. As you quiet your heart and surroundings to hear his voice more, choose to answer God with increasing devotion.

Something to Ponder

The English language distinguishes between the words *listen* and *hear*. In a restaurant, you hear the music on the speakers, chairs scraping, waiters taking orders, and cell phones ringing. Your ears process these sound waves and relegate them to background noise. In the same restaurant, you listen to the voices of those at your table. When God talks to you, will his voice be in the background noise with clattering plates or at the table in intimate conversation?

Digging Deeper

Samuel wasn't the only man or woman chronicled in the Bible who had nocturnal visits from on high. Spend a few minutes reading about the encounters these men had:

- Jacob (Genesis 32:24–30)
- Solomon (1 Kings 3:5–15)
- Joseph (Matthew 1:19–25)
- Peter (Acts 12:3–11)

The Roles of Silence and Solitude

Many arrangements of the hymn "A Mighty Fortress Is Our God" pull out all the stops to blast a marshal anthem of salvation. And yet the psalm on which Martin Luther based his lyrics marches to a different drummer. The psalmist discussed wars, cultural upheaval, and natural disasters, but he quieted the bombast at the end so that you can hear this: "Be still, and know that I am God. . . . The LORD of hosts is with us; the God of Jacob is our refuge" (Psalm 46:10–11 NKJV). Amid noise and deafening silence, God is speaking. Are you listening?

Silence and Solitude

Silence and solitude are the energy drink of an active prayer life. When you shut the door to interruptions and turn down the volume of the culture's messages, you can hear God more clearly. Then you can respond through decisions and actions with greater clarity. Jesus is the best example. Throughout his ministry, Jesus made it his habit to separate himself from the crowds that pressed in. He even pulled apart from his disciples. Jesus needed quiet time alone with his Father.

Being quiet and alone with God fortifies you against temptation. Before Jesus launched his public ministry, the Holy Spirit led him into the desert for forty days of fasting and prayer. This one-on-one boot camp prepared him for the time when Satan would slither up with venomous temptations.

> Rest in God alone, my soul, for my hope comes from Him.
>
> Psalm 62:5 HCSB
>
> When you pray, go away by yourself, shut the door behind you, and pray to your Father in private. Then your Father, who sees everything, will reward you.
>
> Matthew 6:6 NLT

Renewal

*B*eing *quiet and alone with God renews your mind and body.* One night, the whole town went to see Jesus. Jesus healed many. Then, the book of Mark tells us, "very early in the morning, while it was still dark, Jesus got up, left the house and went off to a solitary place, where he prayed" (1:35 NIV). When he saw the disciples again, Jesus led them in a new direction.

When the soldiers went to arrest Jesus, they found him in a garden where he had been alone and in prayer. Jesus was prepared for the darkest days of his ministry.

Something to Ponder

M any Eastern religions encourage silence and solitude. Their meditation practices instruct you to empty your mind. For the Christian, silence and solitude are about filling your soul. After his forty-day fast in the desert and the temptations that followed, "Jesus returned to Galilee in the power of the Spirit" (Luke 4:14 NIV). He was filled, not parched. Fill yourself in his presence.

Digging Deeper

S chedule four hours within the next two weeks when you can take a spiritual retreat. Carry your Bible, a journal, and a pen to a quiet spot at a local park. As you read and pray, thousands of thoughts will interrupt. Write them down quickly and ask God to quiet your heart. Many who have taken similar retreats report that  after the first hour, mental static went away and allowed them to commune with God.

Common Misconceptions About Prayer

The online encyclopedia Wikipedia counters more than 150 common misconceptions about history, science, technology, and other subjects with facts including the following:

- Napoleon Bonaparte was taller than the average nineteenth-century Frenchman.

- Most herbal "teas" contain no tea leaves.

- The North Star is not the brightest star in the northern hemisphere.

- Thomas Edison did not invent the lightbulb.

Similarly, there are probably as many misconceptions about prayer as there are about those who pray, but a lie heard often is still a lie. Three prayer traps seem to snag many Christians, even those who would consider themselves prayer veterans.

✳

The Vending Machine Trap

Whatever I ask God for, God will give to me. This is the most common misconception about prayer. We must consult the whole counsel of God to understand what Jesus meant when he said, "If you remain in Me and My words remain in you, ask whatever you want and it will be done for you" (John 15:7 HCSB). All four Gospels include Jesus' words regarding prayer requests (Matthew 7:7; Mark 11:24; Luke 11:9; and John 15:7), but John expanded on the teaching to bring clarity to the lesson.

In context, Jesus was teaching how

When you ask, you do not receive, because you ask with wrong motives, that you may spend what you get on your pleasures.

James 4:3 NIV

The LORD said to Samuel, "Do not look at his appearance or at the height of his stature, because I have rejected him; for God sees not as man sees, for man looks at the outward appearance, but the LORD looks at the heart."

1 Samuel 16:7 NASB

to build a relationship with him. He is the main vine of a vineyard; you are a branch growing from that main vine, which sprouts grapes. God, the vinedresser, prunes you so that you can produce more fruit. Jesus then made an "if/then/so that" statement: *if* you continue to be connected to me, *then* I will answer your prayers, *so that* you can produce more grapes.

Pastor and author John Piper concluded that "if you want God to respond to your interests, you must be devoted to his interests. God is God. He does not run the world by hiring the consulting firm called Mankind. He lets mankind share in the running of the world through prayer to the degree that we consult with him and get our goals and desires in tune with his purposes."

God is not a vending machine; you can't insert your prayer in the slot, punch a button, and collect your prayer through the door below. By the same token, God is never out of order or out of stock. God loves you and wants to be in an intimate relationship with you so that he can pour out the riches of his kingdom upon you.

The Eloquence Trap

If I pray with multisyllabic words and poetic phrases, God will give my prayers greater priority. Muslims are not allowed to pray in any language but Arabic because their god listens only to prayers spoken in what they believe to be the holy language.

The Bible does not instruct you to pray in a certain language or a certain style. God simply says, "Pray to me" (Jeremiah 29:12 NIV).

Pastor and beloved author A. W. Tozer (1897-1963) tripped into the Eloquence Trap often. "When I am praying the most eloquently," he wrote, "I am getting the least accomplished in my prayer life. But when I stop getting eloquent, give God less theology, shut up, just gaze upward, and wait for God to speak to my heart, he speaks with such power that I have to grab a pencil and a notebook and take notes on what God is saying to my heart."

The Creator and King of the universe deserves your respect, awe, and worship, but no one in heaven or on earth knows you better or loves you more than he does. In essence, you have God at hello.

The Stopwatch Trap

If I pray long enough, God will have to respond. Solomon wisely advised, "In the multitude of words sin is not lacking, but he who restrains his lips is wise" (Proverbs 10:19 NKJV). Many strive to "pray without ceasing" (1 Thessalonians 5:17 NKJV) with many long prayers. This concept has more to do with striving to maintain a spirit of prayer throughout each day.

> When you are praying, do not use meaningless repetition as the Gentiles do, for they suppose that they will be heard for their many words.
>
> Matthew 6:7 NASB

Poet and theologian François de Fénelon (1651–1715) wrote, "Prayer is not made great by a lot of words, for God knows your inmost feelings before you say them. True prayers come from the spirit. You pray only for what you really desire. You could pass whole days 'praying,' but if you do not pray from your deepest, inmost desires, you are not praying."

Pray as long as you need to in order to pour out your heart. Persist in prayer like the widow in Luke 18, but don't filibuster.

Something to Ponder

Misconceptions can be pressed into the fabric of our lives like brands into leather. When facing a misconception, it is sometimes helpful to trace the history of your knowledge on a topic. Spend a few minutes thinking about how you came to believe your misconception about prayer. Then ask God in prayer to help you embrace the truth.

The most effective way to overcome misconceptions is to understand the truth. That's the purpose of this book. This chart highlights Jesus' teaching on prayer.

Jesus' Teaching on Prayer

Passage	Topic
Matthew 6:5-8	Pray naturally
Matthew 6:9-15	The model prayer
Matthew 7:7-11	Asking in prayer
Matthew 18:20	Jesus' promise of his presence
Mark 6:46	Jesus' practical model
Mark 11:24	Believing in prayer
Mark 11:25	Barriers to prayer
Luke 11:1	Jesus' practical model
Luke 18:1-8	Persist in prayer
Luke 18:9-14	Pray with humility
Luke 21:36	Pray for yourself
Luke 22:41-42	Praying in submission
John 14:13-14	Praying in Jesus' name
John 15:7	Pray in relationship
John 16:23-24	Praying in Jesus' name
John 17:9-26	Jesus' prayer for you

Common Barriers to Prayer

Prayer is sometimes like a journey through a construction zone. Potholes jar your body as your car bounces through. A flag-waving construction worker cuts you off. Orange barrels narrow the road, and large wooden signs announce a detour. You wish you could turn your car into a helicopter to fly over it all or just go back to bed and forget the entire trip. What detours—or derails—your prayers? Most barriers fall into two categories: "I" barriers and "God" barriers. This chapter addresses the "I" barriers and the next chapter will cover the "God" barriers.

✳

"I Am Busy"

No matter how busy you are, you always have time for one thing—a crisis. Crises come when you least expect them. They storm into your life, laying waste to your schedule. Crises bring crystal clear clarity to the essentials and priorities of life. You have no choice but to fit a crisis into your life. What if you treated prayer with the same respect as a crisis?

Pastor and renowned church growth specialist Bill Hybels observed that we are trained to believe that time is money, but that the training leads to some dangerous behaviors. Hybels wrote, "The archenemy of spiritual authenticity is busyness, which is closely tied to something the Bible calls *worldliness*—getting caught up with the society's agenda, objectives, and activities to the neglect of walking with God. Anyway you cut it, a key ingredient in authentic Christianity is time. Not leftover time, not throwaway time, but quality time. Time for contemplation, meditation, and reflection. Unhurried, uninterrupted time."

> Be careful how you walk, not as unwise men but as wise, making the most of your time, because the days are evil.
>
> Ephesians 5:15–16 NASB
>
> I have tried hard to find you—don't let me wander from your commands.
>
> Psalm 119:10 NLT

So how do you cut a swath across your schedule to accommodate prayer? The high school and college campus organization Fellowship of Christian Athletes uses a sports metaphor. Leaders encourage the student-athletes to go "first and ten" with God. Spend ten minutes in prayer each morning as the first part of your routine. This technique isn't for "the entire game" but just to get you started. You will seek to increase the minutes once you feel the benefits of committed time to pray.

"I Am Distracted"

Those who have many distractions have many things to pray for. There are two major types of distractions: internal and external.

Internal distractions are thoughts and feelings that captivate your mind. When you quiet yourself for prayer, these gremlins turn up the volume to get your attention. To combat these internal distractions, create a list of all your concerns. Use that list as your guide until you experience a time of prayer not marred by random thoughts.

External distractions include ringing telephones and interrupting children. Electronic devices are easy to disable or unplug. Moms in particular struggle when their children disrupt their times of prayer. They've overcome the barrier of being too busy, but as soon as they take a deep breath, a child needs help. Children require care and attention. Many moms report that they need to wake up before their children do or put the to-do list on hold during naptime in order to pray for just a few minutes without distraction.

"I Am Sleepy"

If bowing your head is a better cure for insomnia than counting sheep, perhaps your environment is more conducive to sleep than it is to prayer. Classic paintings and the monastic life have been combined with the solemnity of prayer to create an expectation that prayer is best when on your knees in silence.

That might work for some Christians at times. Silence and solitude are positive elements to your spiritual life. However, prayer can be just as meaningful while out for a morning run or an afternoon walk. If you have a long commute, spend part of your time in prayer. Keep a 3" x 5" card full of prayer requests behind your visor. One young businessman likes to pray aloud, so he wears his earphones so that it appears he's on a telephone call. In essence, he is talking over the communication line that's never busy.

> Seek first his kingdom and his righteousness, and all these things will be given to you as well.
>
> Matthew 6:33 NIV

"I Am Inadequate"

Even those who have prayed for years feel inadequate from time to time. This barrier rears its head when the basics become dusty. If you feel this way, remind yourself that prayer is simply having a conversation with God.

Something to Ponder

French theologian François de Fénelon once tutored an unruly seven-year-old boy. Their relationship thrived, and the boy became a responsible young man. Years later, Fénelon wrote to his former protégé, "An active personality, accustomed to lots of activity, will faint in solitude. For a long time you have been distracted by much outward activity. By being fruitful you will gradually come to experience a deeper inward life with fewer distractions." Persist in prayer.

Final Thoughts

The most troublesome "I" barrier to prayer is "I Don't Want to Pray." Many are afraid to admit this core thought and choose to voice other barriers that seem more "religiously correct." When you feel this way, ask yourself how God has disappointed you or frustrated you, and then take your feelings to him. King David, the apostle Paul, and many others complained to God. When they did, God drew them closer to himself.

Points to Remember

• People have no choice but to make time for a crisis, and yet many crises could be averted or better handled if people made time for prayer.

• Until you find a way to handle distractions, you can use them as a springboard to prayer.

• If you find that prayer lulls you to sleep, pray when you're most alert or when you can't fall asleep, such as when you're walking or driving.

Difficult Questions About Prayer

Prayer doesn't always come easily. People wonder about why and how they should pray. The good news is that the Bible has the answer for any of your questions about prayer.

Contents

If you have faith when you pray, you will be given whatever you ask for.

Matthew 21:22 CEV

"Why Would God Listen to Me?"

Have you ever heard yourself say, "God doesn't have time for my prayers" or "God doesn't care about my prayers"? Questions like these—the "God" barriers—often arise from past disappointment or misunderstanding. You can get past the "God" barriers by realigning your view of God. Imagine your perception of God as the Leaning Tower of Pisa. You must get under the foundation and repair the balance in order to move forward and into a deeper relationship with God through prayer.

✳

God Wants to Listen to You Because He Loves You

When God instructed Moses to bring his laws to Israel, Moses shared some opening remarks. He said, "The LORD loved your ancestors and wanted them to belong to him. So he chose them and their descendants rather than any other nation, and today you are still his people" (Deuteronomy 10:15 CEV). Inspirational author Max Lucado explained the meaning of the Hebrew word for *love* used here. "This passage warms our hearts. But it shook the Hebrews' world. They heard this: 'The Lord binds [*hasaq*] himself to his people.' *Hasaq* speaks of a tethered love. God chained himself to Israel. Because the people were lovable? No. God loves Israel and the rest of us because he chooses to."

GOD wasn't attracted to you and didn't choose you because you were big and important—the fact is, there was almost nothing to you. He did it out of sheer love, keeping the promise he made to your ancestors.

Deuteronomy 7:7–8 MSG

I do not pray for these alone, but also for those who will believe in Me through their word; that they all may be one, as You, Father, are in Me, and I in You; that they also may be one in Us, that the world may believe that You sent Me.

John 17:20–21 NKJV

God Wants to Listen to You Because He Prays for You

Have you ever had a friend reach out his hand to your shoulder, bow his head, and pour out prayers to God on your behalf? This hopeful and encouraging act of friendship is trumped by only one thing: Jesus himself praying for you. The apostle Paul told the Romans that Jesus "is at God's right side, speaking to him for us" (Romans 8:34 CEV). Jesus is leaning toward his Father, his hands are cupped around his mouth, and he is talking about you directly into God's ear. God listens to you because he listens to his Son.

Final Thoughts

Ambrose (339?-397), a leader in the early church, mused that praying is like a little child who gathers flowers to present to her father. The child picks as many weeds as flowers. The mother snags the child and transforms the bunch into a beautiful bouquet. The prince of preachers, Charles Spurgeon, commented on Ambrose's analogy: "If we could see one of our prayers after Christ Jesus has amended it—we would hardly recognize it."

Something to Ponder

In his teens, George Matheson's eyesight began failing. University and seminary were excruciating. He was blind by graduation. His fiancée returned the engagement ring. He enjoyed a full career as a pastor, but he suffered from a broken heart. Reflecting on God's love, he penned this hymn: "O Love that wilt not let me go, I rest my weary soul in thee; I give thee back the life I owe, that in thine ocean depths its flow may richer, fuller be."

"If God Knows Everything, Why Should I Pray?"

Ken Jennings is probably the only person in history who deserves the title "know-it-all." He reigned as champion on the television game show *Jeopardy* for seventy-four programs and won more money than any regular-season contestant. Some Christians feel as if life is a game of *Jeopardy* played against the God of the universe. They wonder why they should play when God knows all the answers on the board. His infinite knowledge is an invitation to move you closer to him.

✳

God Does Know It All

God is *omniscient*. This theological term means "all knowing." The Bible says that God knows such things as the number of hairs on your head, the stars in the sky, and the grains of sand.

God knows far more than trivial facts about you. He knows your thoughts, plans, and emotions. Jesus traveled on a journey from Judea to his hometown of Galilee. He paused to rest beside a well in Samaria. A woman came to the well, and Jesus spoke to her. Her jaw scraped the sand as Jesus told her about her life and her mistakes and then helped her see him as the Messiah. After her encounter, she ran into town, telling everyone, "Come, see a man who told me everything I ever did! Could this be the Messiah?" (John 4:29 HCSB).

My frame was not hidden from You, when I was made in secret, and skillfully wrought in the depths of the earth; Your eyes have seen my unformed substance; and in Your book were all written the days that were ordained for me, when as yet there was not one of them.

Psalm 139:15–16 NASB

Remember the former things of old, for I am God, and there is no other; I am God, and there is none like Me, declaring the end from the beginning, and from ancient times things that are not yet done, saying, "My counsel shall stand, and I will do all My pleasure."

Isaiah 46:9–10 NKJV

God Does Know Everything, but You Don't

A wise man once said, "God does not tell you everything you will encounter in life. If he did, you would go off and do it without him." God wants a relationship with you. Keep in mind that prayer is dialogue, not monologue. When you pray, you tell God the things you want him to hear. You ask for the things that you need. In reply, God tells you about himself and outlines his plans for you.

Pray in times of doubt and fear. Ask God every question you've ever wondered about. Stay close to him. If life is a test, he knows the answers.

Something to Ponder

Theologian and pastor R. C. Sproul teaches that God's knowledge is different from a human's. He wrote, "God's omniscience, like His omnipotence and omnipresence, also relates to time. God's knowledge is absolute in the sense that He is forever aware of all things. God's intellect is different from ours in that He does not have to 'access' information, like a computer might retrieve a file. All knowledge is always directly before God."

Key Verses on the Omniscience of God

Verse	Aspect of Omniscience
Psalm 147:5	Infinite understanding
Ezekiel 11:5	God's knowledge of your mind
Romans 11:33–36	The mind of God
Acts 15:18	God's eternalness
Hebrews 4:13	What God can see

"Does Prayer Move Me, or Do I Move God in Prayer?"

Jonah had a problem. Jonah was an Old Testament prophet sent by God to the city of Nineveh. God commanded him, "Go to the great city of Nineveh and preach against it, because their wickedness has confronted Me" (Jonah 1:2 HCSB). God was going to wipe out one of the enemies of God's people. Jonah probably felt like you would if God sent you to the Nazis. He also worried that if God heard their prayers, he wouldn't destroy the city. He worried that God might be moved to change his mind.

✴

What Happened in Nineveh

Instead of going to Nineveh, Jonah fled to the sea. The crew threw Jonah overboard to save themselves from a wrathful storm. Jonah was swallowed by a big fish, and he repented of his disobedience. The fish ejected Jonah onto dry land, and Jonah traveled immediately to Nineveh.

Jonah preached that in forty days, God would destroy Nineveh. Word of Jonah's warning reached the king, who ripped his clothes and decreed that all the citizens should repent and pray to the God of Israel for mercy.

Jonah's worst fears came true. "God saw their works, that they turned from their evil way; and God

> God is not man, one given to lies, and not a son of man changing his mind. Does he speak and not do what he says? Does he promise and not come through?
>
> Numbers 23:19 MSG

> The word of the LORD came to Isaiah: "Go and tell Hezekiah that this is what the LORD God of your ancestor David says: I have heard your prayer; I have seen your tears. Look, I am going to add 15 years to your life."
>
> Isaiah 38:4–5 HCSB

relented from the disaster that He had said He would bring upon them, and He did not do it" (Jonah 3:10 NKJV). Because of their prayers, God did not punish this group of people.

Seminary professor and theologian Wayne Grudem explained it this way: "These instances should be all understood as true expressions of God's *present* attitude or intention *with respect to the situation as it exists at that moment.* If the situation changes, then of course God's attitude or expression of intention will also change. This is just saying that God *responds differently to different situations.*"

Conversely, think about Egypt during the days of Moses. Moses and Aaron stood before Pharaoh eleven times. Even when Pharaoh relented and released the Israelites, he didn't show sorrow or repentance. His heart was hard. God brought about his original plan—the delivery of his people. Pharaoh's kingdom received no relief. Eleven times destruction followed Pharaoh's refusal to let God's people go. God brought about ten plagues and then the destruction of the military in the Red Sea. The circumstances did not change, so God brought about the plan as he communicated to Moses.

How This Truth Affects Your Prayers

Jonah warned the people of Nineveh, who in turn begged God to relent and not destroy their civilization. Another prophet, Isaiah, confronted King Hezekiah. Isaiah told him to get his house in order because he would die soon. Hezekiah responded in prayer, repenting and pleading for God's mercy. God extended Hezekiah's life by fifteen years.

God probably will not send a prophet to your doorstep with a specific message of doom. Instead, look to your circumstances. If you continue to make similar decisions and act in similar ways, what is the most likely outcome? If your answer to that question makes your knees knock, cry out to God and ask for mercy.

Remind God of His Promises

The Israelites had front-row tickets to the hard-hearted behavior of Pharaoh and the consequences that rained down on Egypt. However, many years later in the wilderness, their hearts started to calcify. God told Moses to duck because he had grown tired of their behavior and disbelief.

Instead of covering his head with his arms, Moses asked God for mercy. He reminded God of his covenant with his people. Had God forgotten the promises he had made to Abraham, Isaac, Jacob, and all their descendants? Of course not. By reminding God of his words, Moses heard the promise and reminded himself that God keeps his promises. You can do the same in your prayers. Remind God of the truths you've learned from reading the Bible.

> Moses sought the favor of the LORD his God. . . . "Remember your servants Abraham, Isaac and Israel, to whom you swore by your own self: 'I will make your descendants as numerous as the stars in the sky and I will give your descendants all this land I promised them, and it will be their inheritance forever.'" Then the LORD relented and did not bring on his people the disaster he had threatened.
>
> Exodus 32:11, 13–14 NIV

Does God Move You, or Do You Move God in Prayer?

You are moved because you move toward God in relationship. God is moved because his ultimate desire is a deeper relationship with you. Through prayer, your outlook on your circumstances changes as you see through God's eyes. Through prayer, your circumstances change and God then acts based on the new circumstances.

There are dozens of promises within the pages of the Bible. The following chart is merely a partial list for reference.

The Promises of God

Promise	Old Testament Passage	New Testament Passage
God will comfort your fear.	Deuteronomy 31:8	James 4:8
God will give you wisdom.	Psalm 32:8	John 14:26
God will forgive.	2 Chronicles 7:14	1 John 1:9
God will provide.	Genesis 22:14	1 John 5:14–15
God knows the future.	Jeremiah 29:11	John 16:33

Check Your Understanding

- **What criteria does God use to decide between carrying out his original plan and changing according to different circumstances?**

God always remains consistent within his character. God is eternal, holy, unchanging, infinite, all-powerful, all-knowing, self-existent, self-sufficient, merciful, just, gracious, and sovereign.

- **How does God remain consistent in his character yet seemingly change his behavior?**

Here's an example: God cannot tolerate sin. If you break God's rules, he will not let you into heaven. He sent Jesus to earth to pay for your sins. When Jesus died on the cross, the circumstances changed, and thus God's attitude toward you changed.

- **What can I do when I struggle to believe this truth?**

Proverbs 3:5-6 offers great advice: "Trust in the LORD with all your heart and lean not on your own understanding; in all your ways acknowledge him, and he will make your paths straight" (NIV).

"When God Closes a Door, Does He Really Open a Window?"

Imagine a little boy asking his father, "Daddy, may I please have some popcorn?" The father extends a plain brown paper bag. The bag is too high for the boy to see into, so he must reach his hand over the rim of the bag. He feels inside and pulls out the contents. What does he remove? The potential answers to this question illustrate how God answers our prayers. God always hears your prayers and always responds. His responses can be divided into four categories: (1) yes, (2) no, (3) later, and (4) something better.

✳

If the father said yes to his son's request, the boy would have reached in to find warm kernels of popped corn. If the father had said no, the son would have felt only air. If the father had planned to delay his yes, the son would have found a handful of unpopped kernels. And if the father had wan ted to exceed his son's expectations, the child would have discovered caramel popcorn, cheese popcorn, or kettle popcorn.

"Yes!"

God revels in answering his children's prayers. The people of God rejoiced when he answered their prayers. They often gave God

> When the servant of the man of God got up early the next morning and went outside, there were troops, horses, and chariots everywhere. "Oh, sir, what will we do now?" the young man cried to Elisha. "Don't be afraid!" Elisha told him. "For there are more on our side than on theirs!" Then Elisha prayed, "O LORD, open his eyes and let him see!" The LORD opened the young man's eyes, and when he looked up, he saw that the hillside around Elisha was filled with horses and chariots of fire.
>
> 2 Kings 6:15–17 NLT

a new name to celebrate his intervention. These terms of endearment became spoken reminders of the faithfulness of God.

One of the most poignant yes answers came when Abraham trudged up Mount Moriah to sacrifice his son Isaac (Genesis 22). Abraham surely questioned why, but moved forward anyway. He told Isaac, "God will provide for Himself the lamb for a burnt offering" (v. 8 NKJV). Abraham must have prayed with every step. When Isaac was bound, he must have prayed for a substitute with every huffing breath. The Lord waited until Abraham lifted the knife before telling an angel to shout, "Abraham!" Abraham loosed Isaac, and together they sacrificed the ram stuck in the thorns. They called the place Jehovah-Jireh—"The LORD Will Provide (v. 14 NIV).

"No!"

God also says no to prayer requests. The negative response often produces doubt, disappointment, or anger. When God says no, remember that he is acting in your best interest. When you ask why and receive no answers, remember that he loves you and is protecting you.

He might have said no to you in the same way he refused Jim's request. Jim's car died on the way to a job interview. As he watched the news that evening, he marveled at the report of a fatal accident a few blocks and a few minutes from where his car broke down. He wondered if he might have been the victim instead.

On the night before his crucifixion, Jesus agonized in prayer at the garden of Gethsemane. The Bible tells us that he sweat blood, a condition that occurs only under the heaviest stress. He asked, "O My Father, if it is possible, let this cup pass from Me" (Matthew 26:39 NKJV). The cup equaled his execution on the cross. God said no and Jesus was crucified. God acted in the best interest of all creation. Jesus had to die so that God could carry out his plan to rescue humankind.

"Later!"

God's eternalness is one of his most amazing attributes. He can see across the arc of time. He sees the whole of his grand story. God may be more than willing to grant your request, but he may see a better time for your prayer to come to fruition.

> Your father's blessings are greater than the blessings of the ancient mountains, than the bounty of the age-old hills.
>
> Genesis 49:26 NIV

The prophets foretold the Messiah's birth for hundreds of years before Jesus arrived. The apostle Paul told us, "When the fullness of the time came, God sent forth His Son, born of a woman, born under the Law" (Galatians 4:4 NASB). A modern-day proverb quips, "God is seldom early, but never late."

"Something Better!"

God longs to bless his children. The apostle Paul discussed the amazing riches of God's kingdom. You can almost hear him growing louder and more excited with each sentence until he proclaimed, "To him who is able to do immeasurably more than all we ask or imagine, according to his power that is at work within us, to him be glory in the church and in Christ Jesus throughout all generations, for ever and ever! Amen" (Ephesians 3:20–21 NIV).

God longs to pour out the riches of his kingdom into your life. He surprises his children. When God closes a door (says no), sometimes he opens a window. And sometimes he takes the whole roof off.

Something to Ponder

When Jesus prayed in the garden of Gethsemane, he closed with the words "Nevertheless, not as I will, but as You will" (Matthew 26:39 NKJV). God's will supersedes your will. All of his answers—yes, no, later, and something better—come from his master plan. The key to accepting any of the four answers is trust. No matter what answer you receive to your request, trust that God knows what he's doing.

Old Testament Names Celebrating God's Attributes and Character

Name	English Translation	Scripture
Adonai	Lord (as a title)	Isaiah 6:1–8
El-Elyon	Most High God Sovereign Ruler	Isaiah 14:13–15
El-Gibborim	Mighty God	Isaiah 9:6
Elohim Tsebhaoth	Lord of Hosts	Jeremiah 11:20
Elohim	God Mighty One Powerful	Genesis 1:1–24
El-Olam	Everlasting God	Isaiah 40:28
El-Roi	God Who Sees	Genesis 16:13
El-Shaddai	God Almighty All-Sufficient One	Genesis 17:1
Jehovah-Jireh	God Will Provide	Genesis 22:14
Jehovah-M'Kaddish	God Sanctifies	Leviticus 20:7–8
Jehovah–Nissi	God, My Banner God, My Victory	Exodus 17:15
Jehovah-Rapha	God Heals	Exodus 15:26
Jehovah-Rohi	God, My Shepherd Tender Relationship	Psalm 23:1
Jehovah-Sabaoth	Lord of Hosts Strong Tower	1 Samuel 1:3–11
Jehovah-Shalom	God Is Our Peace	Judges 6:24
Jehovah-Shammah	God Is Present	Ezekiel 48:35
Jehovah-Tsidkem	God Our Righteousness	Jeremiah 23:5–6
Tsue	Rock	Deuteronomy 32:4
Yahweh	Lord I Am Self-Existent	Exodus 3:1–14

"The Situation Is Impossible, So Why Should I Pray?"

Old scholars trying to trip up those who believe in the Bible used to ask, "If God can do anything, can he make a rock so large that he cannot move it?" The answer to this riddle helps us understand the nature of prayer: God can do nothing against his nature. For example, God cannot allow a sinner who has not repented into heaven. The converse is also true; God cannot prevent a sinner who has repented from enering heaven. Rejoice because God's nature includes miracles, wonders, and doing the impossible.

Pray to Feel the Comfort of God

King Saul hunted David like an animal. The future king hid in the brush or rocks, dodging soldiers who came within a spear's length of finding him. For months, the Lord preserved him. David composed Psalm 31 to celebrate God's protection and safety. When life feels impossible and storms rage around you, go to God in prayer for his protection and comfort.

> I know what it is to be in need, and I know what it is to have plenty. I have learned the secret of being content in any and every situation, whether well fed or hungry, whether living in plenty or in want. I can do everything through him who gives me strength.
>
> Philippians 4:12–13 NIV

Pray Because God Weeps with You

Where was Jesus? Sisters Mary and Martha were losing their patience. Their brother was dying, but Jesus was busy in the neighboring town. Didn't Jesus care? Wasn't Lazarus his friend? When Jesus finally arrived, the sisters met him with the news: Lazarus was dead. Jesus wept with them. In a matter of minutes, Jesus would raise Lazarus from the grave. Nevertheless, Jesus wept. When your grief and sorrow are at their worst, go to God in prayer because he weeps with you.

Pray Because God Can Do the Impossible

Moses passed the mantle of leadership to Joshua. It was then up to him to lead Israel into the Promised Land. Could God do the impossible again? Five times, God told Joshua to be strong and courageous. God prepared him for challenges and difficulty. Then God did the impossible—he divided the Jordan River. A second crossing. A second miracle. When the impossible stares you in the face, pray because God can do the impossible.

Jesus is the Lord of the impossible. When you're facing the impossible, find encouragement in Jesus' miracles.

Jesus' Miracles

Nature	Matthew 21:18-19; Mark 4:35-41; Luke 4:28-30; 5:4-11; John 2:1-12; 6:15-21; 21:1-14
Healing	Matthew 8:1-4; 9:18-26, 27-31; 12:9-14; 15:21-28; Mark 1:29-31; 7:31-37 8:22-26; Luke 5:17-26; 7:1-10, 11-17; 13:10-17; 14:1-6; 17:11-19; 22:50-51; John 4:46-54; 5:1-15; 9:1-12
Resurrection	Mark 5:21-24, 35-43; John 11:38-44; 21:1-14
Demons	Matthew 8:28-34; 12:22; Mark 1:21-28;
Wonders	Matthew 15:32-39; 17:1-13, 24-27; Luke 2:42-51; John 6:1-14

Practical Matters of Prayer

Once the larger questions are answered, others that are more practical in nature but just as important begin to surface. What you need is a how-to manual for different situations.

Contents

When his people pray for help, he listens
and rescues them from their troubles.

Psalm 34:17 CEV

How to Pray Aloud

Glossaphobia **is the fear of speaking in public. Some surveys contend that more than 70 percent of Americans fear speaking in front of others more than they fear dying. As Christians, this social fear shows up when praying aloud in the presence of other believers. Don't let your fear keep you away from experiencing the great joy. Whether praying with a small group of others or opening a meeting in prayer, keep these things in common.**

✵

Pray for God's Ears Alone

Even though there may be a few—or a few dozen—others in the room, direct your words to the ears of God alone. Avoid the temptation to perform. Christians in South Korea pray aloud, but they don't take turns the way Christians in America do; everyone prays aloud simultaneously. This practice helps focus their prayers toward heaven and tamps down ego.

Avoid Using Prayer to Curse Others

When David was fighting war after war, he often prayed against his enemies. These petitions (such as Psalm 35) are called imprecatory (i.e., cursing) prayers. While most prayers are good models, impreca-

About midnight Paul and Silas were praying and singing hymns of praise to God, and the prisoners were listening to them; and suddenly there came a great earthquake, so that the foundations of the prison house were shaken; and immediately all the doors were opened and everyone's chains were unfastened.

Acts 16:25–26 NASB

Let us not neglect our meeting together, as some people do, but encourage one another, especially now that the day of his return is drawing near.

Hebrews 10:25 NLT

tory prayers should never be heard in public. Conflict exists in every group, but the prayer circle is not an appropriate place to air your grievances.

Avoid Verbal Traps

Praying aloud is a unique speaking experience. In public speaking, some people fall on such verbal crutches as *um, you see, and, etc., and all that*. When praying aloud, some use these crutches and add others, like using God's name to begin or connect sentences. Remember to speak as naturally as possible.

Something to Ponder

Moses suffered from a fear of public speaking. He complained to God about the task, his lack of eloquence, and even the sound of his voice. God's response to Moses is a great reminder when you worry about praying in public. "Who gave man his mouth? Who makes him deaf or mute? Who gives him sight or makes him blind? Is it not I, the LORD?" (Exodus 4:11 NIV).

Myth Buster

Have you heard that women aren't allowed to pray aloud if men are present? Christian traditions debate the roles of men and women in public worship. Some advocate for a woman's silence by quoting 1 Corinthians 14:34: "Women should remain silent in the churches. They are not allowed to speak, but must be in submission"  (NIV). A more complete reading of the New Testament gives women great freedom in public worship—including praying aloud—but reserves teaching for men only.

How to Pray in a Group

The practice of praying together originated in the first gathering of believers after the ascension of Jesus Christ to heaven. The book of Acts records exciting and transformative events. While the apostles waited for Pentecost, they gathered in a room with other close followers. The activities of these early gatherings included listening to the apostles' teaching, spending time and sharing meals with one another, and praying for one another's needs. When you pray with a group, you are continuing an unbroken chain from the days of the New Testament.

✳

Praying in a group should be as natural as conversation. Throughout the centuries, habits and unofficial rules have shaped the way groups pray. These practical guidelines help make group prayer more meaningful and natural, but they shouldn't become legalistic requirements.

How to Take Prayer Requests

Many groups begin their prayer time by soliciting prayer requests. This custom communicates the details and the story behind a request. Requests should be offered in an attitude of reverence. Some requests can become announcements or gossip. Check your motives before you add your request to the list.

Appoint a scribe to write down and distribute prayer requests. A list allows members to pray for one another throughout the time

> These all with one mind were continually devoting themselves to prayer, along with the women, and Mary the mother of Jesus, and with His brothers.
>
> Acts 1:14 NASB
>
> They were continually devoting themselves to the apostles' teaching and to fellowship, to the breaking of bread and to prayer.
>
> Acts 2:42 NASB

between meetings. It also becomes a living document. Brief notes about how God answered the prayers broaden your group's journal. You can see the hand of God moving in your midst. Log the dates of the requests and the answers.

Taking prayer requests can burn precious time intended for actual prayer. Fern Nichols, founder of Moms in Touch, encourages her chapters to spend the majority of their time together in prayer. If a group desires to keep a journal, they have the freedom to take notes during prayer.

Unspoken Requests

Since God knows everything, he knows the hearts and needs of the members of your group. Everyone should feel open and free to share concerns, but human nature can get in the way. Allow a group member to say, "I have a private request." Others can then reach out to God in prayer on her behalf. This routine also opens up prayer opportunities about confidential matters.

The Health Rut

Asking for prayer can sometimes feel like inviting a camera crew from a reality TV show into your life. Groups often gravitate toward safe requests such as physical health. Everyone experiences health problems from time to time.

Do not forsake praying for health needs. There are serious health concerns that should be a part of the fabric of your group's prayer life such as cancer, a problem pregnancy, and trauma. Chronic conditions such as Alzheimer's, autism, and arthritis should not be overlooked. The admonition is to pray for "health and more," not health alone.

If you are facilitating the prayer time for your group, consider asking questions to help your group pray for a wider variety of needs: Is anyone praying for the salvation of someone? Is anyone struggling with a relationship issue? Are there any workplace or unemployment issues? Is anyone struggling to trust God with a need?

Giving Everyone Time to Pray

Group dynamics should not distract your group from the focus of your time: talking to and hearing from God. However, prayer time can feel dicey. Questions abound. Is he finished praying yet or is that a pause? Has anyone's request been left out? How long should I wait after she's finished before I begin?

> While Peter was in prison, the church prayed very earnestly for him.
>
> Acts 12:5 NLT

Discuss these issues with your group. The conversation will be insightful and downright funny. Here are a couple of suggestions to ease the tension:

- If your group is small enough, hold hands and pray in order. Person #1 opens in prayer and will close when all are finished. When he is finished, he squeezes the hand of #2. If #2 doesn't want to pray aloud, she then squeezes the hand of #3. This continues around the circle until #1 closes.

- If your group is larger, two members might begin praying at the same time. Just laugh it off. A shrewd leader could say, "Anita, why don't you pray first. Then Eric can pray."

Closing in Prayer

The larger the group, the more difficult closing can be. The group leader should designate someone to close in prayer. If your group struggles to end on time, the group leader should feel the freedom to say, "We have time for two more prayers before we close."

Technology has enabled churches and other organizations to distribute prayer requests faster and invite a larger sphere to join in prayer more often. These tech tools are often praised for bringing a church closer together, but have raised some security and privacy concerns.

Technology—Benefits and Cautions

Technology	Benefits	Cautions
Telephone prayer chain	Very personal; communicates urgency and emotion of the need.	Used to be fast, but has been eclipsed by the Internet; some facts can be distorted by repetition.
Blog or MySpace page	Allows detailed description of prayer need; others can pray for and encourage you through commenting.	Very public forum.
Facebook	Limited to your "friends"; allows quick notification and interactive follow-up.	Most users have a wider list of friends than those inclined to pray; friends of yours might repost the request as gossip within their circles.
Twitter	Instantaneous communication; limited to your "followers."	Limited to 140 characters; unless you have a locked profile, others could re-tweet your need beyond your intended scope.
Internet user group (such as Google or Yahoo! groups)	Very private and secure; can offer detailed descriptions; quick notification of requests and responses.	E-mail–driven and may not reach those without mobile devices.

Prayers Online

Many blogs and bulletin boards invite members to offer prayers. If you participate, don't use the opportunity to write a note to the organizer; simply pray to the Father using your computer's keys. Keep your prayers brief so that those being prayed for can skim through all the offered prayers.

How to Open Meetings with Prayer

Worldwide evangelist Franklin Graham caused an international controversy and flurry of lawsuits when he gave an invocation at President George W. Bush's inauguration in 2001. He closed his prayer with, "We pray this in the name of the Father, and of the Son, the Lord Jesus Christ, and of the Holy Spirit. Amen." His prayer exemplifies all the criteria listed below. The firestorm of criticism he received highlights the precarious nature of opening in prayer.

✗

Purpose. Your prayer is more than words. Seek to focus the attention of the group, ask for God's blessing, and set the proper tone.

Tone and Formality. Follow the broadcaster's adage: match emotion with emotion. Consider where the event fits on a spectrum from casual to sacrosanct. The words of your prayer and the tone of your delivery should match your evaluation. Double-check your observations with the organizer.

Length. The length of your prayer should be in direct proportion to the length and importance of the event. For civic groups and awards banquets, twenty to thirty seconds is sufficient (about eighty words). Franklin Graham's inauguration prayer lasted three minutes (about 450 words).

[David] appointed some of the Levites to minister before the ark of the LORD, to commemorate, to thank, and to praise the LORD God of Israel.

1 Chronicles 16:4 NKJV

Solomon stood before the altar of the LORD in front of the entire community of Israel. He lifted his hands toward heaven, and he prayed, "O LORD, God of Israel, there is no God like you in all of heaven above or on the earth below. You keep your covenant and show unfailing love to all who walk before you in wholehearted devotion."

1 Kings 8:22–23 NLT

Dress. Ask about the dress code. If there isn't one, try to match the clothing choice of the emcee or keynote speaker. Clothing choices for special occasions, such as an Eagle Scout Court of Honor, might require extra consideration.

Protocol. At small meetings, stand and offer your prayer from your seat. At larger meetings, you may have a seat at the head table or on the dais. Wait until you are introduced before moving toward the lectern, and then shake the hand of the emcee. Refrain from making opening remarks, but invite those in attendance to join you in prayer. If food is being served, don't forget to return thanks for the meal.

Microphones. Arrive early for a sound check. Speak in a clear voice at medium volume, and let the sound system do the heavy lifting. The sound engineer will make any necessary adjustments.

Myth Buster

Some people think that prayers should not be rehearsed because they are not a performance. However, keep in mind the purpose of your opening prayer: to be an ambassador for God. Your example, tone of voice, word choice, and execution lead the audience in prayer as much as your words. Don't be afraid to rehearse.

Point to Remember

Don't be surprised to see a video camera capturing your event. Inexpensive equipment, local cable networks, and YouTube have created a demand for more video content. Don't offer your prayer in direct address looking straight into the camera. Instead, extend your invitation to the room while slowly looking left and right, and then bow your head. Also, avoid the temptation to look at the camera as you move from your seat to the podium and back again.

Holding Hands for Mealtime Prayers

Today's mealtime prayers look less like a Norman Rockwell painting and more like a television commercial for a casual dining restaurant, and yet families are united throughout the ages by the prayers they've prayed before breaking bread. Food is a consistent part of every day. Our bodies require food to survive. Praying before meals reminds us who provided the food and gives us at least one opportunity each day to express our dependence on the Provider.

An Old Testament Tradition—Thanksgiving

Agriculture fueled much of Israel's calendar. Thanksgiving was integral to the many feasts celebrated each year. They brought sacrifices from their crops and herds to the temple out of thanksgiving and worship. Many of the psalms repeat the refrain of thanksgiving and gratitude.

New Testament Model—Blessing

Jesus modeled a lifestyle of praying before meals. Before two fish and five loaves became an all-you-can-eat buffet, Jesus thanked God for the provision and blessed the food. In the upper room during the Last Supper, Jesus thanked God for the bread and the wine.

Ordering the people to sit down on the grass, [Jesus] took the five loaves and the two fish, and looking up toward heaven, He blessed the food, and breaking the loaves He gave them to the disciples, and the disciples gave them to the crowds.

Matthew 14:19 NASB

I received from the Lord that which I also delivered to you: that the Lord Jesus on the same night in which He was betrayed took bread; and when He had given thanks, He broke it and said, "Take, eat; this is My body which is broken for you; do this in remembrance of Me."

1 Corinthians 11:23–24 NKJV

Practical Matters

Singing Table Prayers. Many families enjoy singing their pre-meal prayers. Enjoy the process and laughter, and know that the practice will help rutabagas taste a little better.

Praying in a Restaurant. While singing isn't recommended, your family's routine is portable to fast-food and sit-down restaurants alike. Prayers should be shorter than at home. If the restaurant isn't teeming with the sounds of clatter, music, and conversation, keep your volume low to avoid distracting other diners.

Teaching Opportunity. Your children can learn to pray in short, fun spurts by praying for your family's meal. Invite the child to do so before you arrive at the table to avoid stage fright. Model how to participate in prayer while your child prays, and thank the child after the prayer. You'll build a spiritual discipline and confidence in your child.

Final Thoughts

The simple act of holding hands transforms mealtime into a solemn, special, and memorable time. In one family, Dad prays while the other members of the family gently squeeze the hands of those next to them to indicate agreement with the prayer. Another family created "shake the love." After the *amen*, everyone raises held hands above their heads and says, "Johnson family: shake the love!" The giggles and smiles lighten even the heaviest days.

Kneeling for Bedtime Prayers

Parents worldwide have struggled with bedtime prayers for generations. Many feel empty merely praying, "Now I lay me down to sleep." They worry that the rote repetition will lead to a lack of interest in spiritual matters as they grow older. Others wonder about the nuts and bolts. They wonder how they can teach their children to pray if they barely know how to pray themselves. Many parents question if bedtime prayers do any good. Bedtime prayers offer six benefits to your child.

☦

Bedtime prayers quiet your child before bedtime. It's hard to fall asleep when you're bouncing on your bed or playing with a toy. Prayer time offers a chance to settle down, be still, and be quiet right before bedtime. The heart rate will slow and, hopefully, the eyelids will begin to droop. This benefit is more practical than spiritual, but it is important nonetheless. For better results, dim the lights and speak in soft tones for a few minutes before prayer time to start the descent.

Bedtime prayers offer you an opportunity to speak into your child's life. Most parents fall into a rut of praying short-sighted prayers, that is, prayers for a good night's sleep or for a good day tomorrow. The prayer model in the Bible asks God for growth in aspects of character over a lifetime. As your child hears you asking God for higher things, you are training your child to desire higher things. C. S. Lewis observed, "We are half-hearted creatures fooling about . . . when infinite joy is offered us, like an ignorant child who wants to go on making mud pies in a slum because he cannot imagine what is meant by the offer of a holiday at the sea. We are far too easily pleased." Pray

> His delight is in the law of the LORD, and in His law he meditates day and night.
>
> Psalm 1:2 NASB
>
> I stay awake through the night, thinking about your promise.
>
> Psalm 119:148 NLT

specifically for traits under development. For instance, if your child is lying, pray for a truthful heart and an end to the lies.

Bedtime prayers give a blanket of godly—and parental—protection. Some children are afraid of the dark. Some are afraid of storms that might stir up overnight. Others are afraid of imaginary creatures tucked away in their closets. Parents fear wars and the rumors of wars, financial stress, traffic accidents, and the unknown. Bedtime prayers remind us that God is in control and help us to look to him for protection and comfort. When your children hear you casting your cares upon the Lord, they will follow with their cares. When you hear yourself casting your cares upon the Lord, your faith will grow.

Bedtime prayers program your child's dreams. Sleep scientists and psychologists report that children dream three or four times every night.

Your child will dream most often about his worries or the last thing on his mind before going to sleep. Bedtime prayers provide tremendous power to shape their dreams. As you pray with your children, you can help them see how God answered their prayers, protected them on the playground, and made their scrapes better. Your prayers for peace will be answered by God and allow your child to experience more dreams than nightmares. If your child does wake up from a bad dream, your prayers can also be the key to getting him back to sleep.

Bedtime prayers allow you to hear from your child's heart. As your child develops language, encourage him to pray along with you. Start with a written prayer like "Now I lay me down to sleep" or the Lord's Prayer. Once your child is comfortable praying aloud with you, coach your child how to talk with God the way your child talks with you. The text of your child's prayer will surprise you and sometimes break your heart. Consider keeping a journal of prayers your child makes and the answers God brings.

Bedtime prayers build family memories. Think back to your own childhood. What do you remember more—the things your family did repeatedly or only once? Many children will remember your family traditions—both good and bad—far more vividly than landmark vacations. Pray as consistently as possible. Some families ask babysitters to keep the tradition going when they can't be at home. Don't rush. Bedtime prayers are an important part of Christian parenting, not just an item on the day's checklist. Linger for a few seconds after the *amen*. If the prayer time generates a question, listen carefully and quietly answer.

> Pray diligently. Stay alert, with your eyes wide open in gratitude.
>
> Colossians 4:2 MSG

Myth Buster

Is it true that children use bedtime prayers to manipulate their parents into staying up later? Many parents struggle to discern whether their children's questions are the genuine thoughts of spiritual growth or a stalling technique. Clear boundaries can aid you. If your child's bedtime is 8:00 and you typically spend five minutes in prayer, begin your prayers at 7:50 so you have time to pray and field questions. When 8:00 comes, remind your child of the family rule. Use discernment if your child seems to be stalling.

Something to Ponder

Don't be afraid to make bedtime prayers fun.

- Does your child sleep with a toy? Add the bear or doll to your prayer circle. Take one hand and ask your child to take the other. Don't forget to pray for the toy by name.

- Sing your prayers by making up your own words to a simple song like "Twinkle, Twinkle, Little Star."

- Hide under a blanket with a flashlight and whisper your prayers.

Final Thoughts

 Do you pray before your bedtime? The same reasons that prayer makes sleep time better for your children will make the evening better for you. Don't allow a stand-up comedian's monologue, an infomercial, or a black-and-white movie to be the last thing on the screen of your mind when you turn out the lights.

Check Your Understanding

- **Can prayer help prevent my child's nightmares?**

Prayer can ward off nightmares in several ways. By making prayer your child's last activity of the night, you make it more likely her dreams will reflect what you prayed about. Praying creates a peaceful atmosphere more conducive to pleasant dreams.

- **Won't my child see this as just another routine in his day?**

If you treat this as a special time and avoid making the prayers themselves routine, your child will likely carry into adulthood precious memories of this family tradition.

How to Use the Bible as a Guide to Effective Prayer

Some of the most profound prayers in history are recorded in the Bible. Two of Jesus' prayers are among the most quoted words worldwide in every language. God's people are a praying people. Since God is the leader, his people follow him and communicate with him. And yet prayer is stronger than a fiber-optic telephone line and faster than a walkie-talkie. The Bible becomes a powerful guide and model for your prayers as you follow God and communicate with him.

✳

The Tone, Attitude, and Content of Biblical Prayers

Imagine having video footage of all the prayers in the Bible edited together in a tight sequence. Watching the prayers back-to-back, you would see a pattern emerge. God's people pray in a personal tone, with a reverent attitude, and they speak blunt words.

- Adam and Eve walked and talked with God in the cool of the day. They talked with him as if he were their neighbor.

- God called Abraham his friend, and yet Abraham prayed with a reverent heart. Many times, Abraham prayed bold prayers without any "spin."

Dear brothers and sisters, I urge you in the name of our Lord Jesus Christ to join in my struggle by praying to God for me.

Romans 15:30 NLT

Listen, GOD! Please, pay attention! Can you make sense of these ramblings, my groans and cries? King-God, I need your help. Every morning you'll hear me at it again. Every morning I lay out the pieces of my life on your altar and watch for fire to descend.

Psalm 5:1–3 MSG

- In Moses' landmark interaction with God, he removed his sandals because he was on holy ground. Reverence marked his prayers, but Moses was not afraid to ask hard things of God.

- David and the other psalmists provided some of the greatest language for your prayers. They demonstrated great agony and joy, sincere devotion, and acute doubt.

- Jesus taught us in the model prayer—known worldwide as the Lord's Prayer—to go to God as a child to her father, a radical concept in Jesus' culture. In his prayer for all believers—the High Priestly Prayer—Jesus prayed with reverence, with familiarity, and wasn't afraid to ask God to be generous to his people.

- The apostle Paul is a great mentor for your personal prayers. In each of his letters, he let you see the content and intent of his own personal prayers.

Even with these great prayers at your disposal, using the Bible as a guide is a daunting task. The Bible is full of history. What one person prays is not necessarily what you should pray. Their lives and circumstances are different from yours. Look more to their hearts and the big picture of what they prayed than to the specific words or requests.

The Bible is God's story of interacting with his people. Adam and Eve were kicked out of the garden of Eden because of their sin. Noah and his family were the only ones to survive the worldwide flood. As you fast-forward through history, Jesus the Ultimate Redeemer came to earth, died for the sins of God's people, and gave us new promises and a new commandment. When you use Old Testament prayers as your model, remind yourself to pray in the light of where God is in his story—after the cross and before heaven.

Getting Started

Use the following suggestions as training wheels for your prayers. The Psalms and the prayers of Paul provide rich content and the fewest mousetraps for your words.

1. Read a phrase or a verse of Scripture.

2. Pray the intent of the phrase or verse in your own words. When praying for someone else, follow the same pattern.

3. Repeat the process for several verses in a row or until the natural end of the passage.

An example of praying for yourself:

- Scripture—"The Lord is my shepherd; there is nothing I lack" (Psalm 23:1 HCSB).

- Prayer—Thank you, Lord, for being my shepherd. Thank you for protecting me and providing for me. Thank you for always being beside me. Even though you're beside me, I'm fearful. I can say like David, "I shall 1 want." Help me to trust y‹ that.

Moses said, "I pray You, show me Your glory!"

Exodus 33:18 NASB

An example of praying for someone else:

- Scripture—"Since the day we heard this, we haven't stopped praying for you. We are asking that you may be filled with the knowledge of His will" (Colossians 1:9 HCSB).

- Prayer—Dear God, please help Jim find a job. He's struggling to keep going. God, please fill him with knowledge of what you want him to do. What should he do today? Help him to make the phone calls, set up meetings, and carry out the follow-up necessary to get a new job.

The passages in the following chart are great places to start your journey of praying with the Bible as your guide.

Prayer Passages in the Bible

Psalms	Letters of Paul
Psalm 1	Romans 1:8–10
Psalm 3	1 Corinthians 1:4–9
Psalms 23–30	2 Corinthians 1:3–11
Psalm 42	Galatians 1:3–5
Psalm 73	Ephesians 1:3–23
Psalm 90	Philippians 1:3–11
Psalm 100	Colossians 1:3–23
Psalm 101	1 Thessalonians 1:2–4
Psalm 127	1 Timothy 2:1–7
Psalm 139	2 Timothy 1:3–14
Psalm 150	Philemon 4–6

Final Thoughts

Spiritual disciplines have been taught through the ages from the early church fathers to modern-day megachurch pastors. Praying the Bible for yourself and for others integrates many of the spiritual disciplines: prayer, Bible reading, Bible study, and Bible meditation. Praying through the Bible is a practice that will encourage your heart and enrich your soul.

The Power of Fasting

Before Jesus took his ministry public, he spent forty days without food and drink. This elongated fast was a time of spiritual preparation for his three years of ministry, healing, teaching, and, ultimately, his sacrificial death on the cross. Since Old Testament times, fasting has been a method chosen by God's people to grow closer to God or to walk through a difficult spiritual season. Here you'll walk through the spiritual implications and practical considerations of fasting. Important to note: several medical conditions preclude fasting, so please consult with your medical professional before beginning a fast of any length. Children should not fast from food.

✳

What Does Fasting Accomplish?

Fasting is a physical parable. When you grow hungry or thirsty for physical sustenance, your body is reminding your soul that you should hunger and thirst for spiritual food and water. Fasting is a method of focusing your attention on the God of the universe.

Why Should You Fast?

You should not fast for the sake of fasting. Fasting in the Bible is always in response to a specific issue, problem, or opportunity:

- Fast to overcome a recurring sin like gossiping or laziness.

- Fast on behalf of a friend facing severe illness.

While they were worshiping the Lord and fasting, the Holy Spirit said, "Set apart for me Barnabas and Saul for the work to which I have called them." So after they had fasted and prayed, they placed their hands on them and sent them off.

Acts 13:2–3 NIV

This is the kind of fasting I want: Free those who are wrongly imprisoned; lighten the burden of those who work for you. Let the oppressed go free, and remove the chains that bind people.

Isaiah 58:6 NLT

- Fast before beginning a new job.

- Fast before making an important decision like buying a house or choosing a spouse.

- Fast for government leaders or military operations.

How Long Should You Fast?

If you have never fasted before, abstain from food for only one meal. Over the next few years, increase the length and frequency of your fasting. Some people fast once a year, while others try to fast once a quarter. Attempt a forty-day fast only after building a routine of fasting in your life.

When Should You Start Your Fast?

When starting with one meal, fast from lunch. If you are employed, reserve the time on your calendar. Sit in your car or drive to a nearby quiet spot for your prayer time. If you're a stay-at-home mom, you might have to feed your children and then involve them in a task or naptime before you can spend time in prayer. Every situation is different and requires creativity and planning. Think ahead about how you will fast, when you will fast, and where you will fast.

If you are fasting for a day or longer, begin your fast with dinner. Practically speaking, you will not grow as hungry in the evening and then can sleep through six or more hours of the worst hunger pangs. Starting with dinner gives you the best opportunity for a longer fast.

What Do You Do When You Fast?

During Mealtime. Fasting without prayer is just a diet. Instead of eating, take your Bible, a notebook, and a pen to a quiet spot. Close your office or bedroom door, drive to a local park, or just sit in your car. Instead of eating food, feast on the Bible and prayer. Study passages related to the purpose of your fast.

The Rest of the Time. Go about life as normally as possible.

When You Feel Hungry. When you feel acute hunger and catch yourself reaching for money for the vending machine, you've just received a signal to pray again. Wherever you are, bow your head and pray for a few seconds, then go back to the task at hand.

> When you fast, do not be like the hypocrites, with a sad countenance. For they disfigure their faces that they may appear to men to be fasting. Assuredly, I say to you, they have their reward. But you, when you fast, anoint your head and wash your face, so that you do not appear to men to be fasting, but to your Father who is in the secret place; and your Father who sees in secret will reward you openly.
>
> Matthew 6:16–18 NKJV

How Do You Break Your Fast?

In the same way that you should begin your fast with the evening meal, you should also break your fast with the evening meal. After going without food for a while, your body's digestive system will kick into high gear and you will feel very sleepy. Consume a small meal at dinner, and then relax before going to sleep.

As a rule of thumb, the longer you fast, the softer your foods should be. If you have fasted for a week or longer, break your fast with clear broth and maybe a few crackers. The next morning, eat oatmeal or an egg. Avoid dairy products like milk on dry cereal or yogurt until the second day.

Jesus' Instructions to Those Who Fast

When Jesus taught the disciples to pray, he shared with them the model prayer—the Lord's Prayer—then gave instructions about fasting. He urged them to not fast publicly. Fasting isn't a spiritual merit badge to be worn; it is a private communion with God. Maintain your normal hygiene and standards of dress. When others invite you to join them for a meal or a trip to a coffee bar, politely decline.

Something to Ponder

It isn't necessary to fast from food. Food is a constant in our lives. For some, coffee, soft drinks, television, video games, or the Internet may feel as required as breathing. These daily indulgences and distractions can be just as difficult to go without as food. If fasting from food is medically prohibited or seems too daunting, you can fast from something like television. Use the same principle: when you would normally watch TV, pray.

Points to Remember

• Do not strenuously exercise—such as train for a marathon—while fasting.

• Drink some clear broth or clear fruit juice during family meals. Use your fast as an opportunity to teach your children about this spiritual discipline.

• When the urge to chew distracts you from prayers or daily life, chew a piece of sugarless gum.

• Limit your water intake to sixty-four ounces a day so you don't overwhelm your kidneys.

Digging Deeper

The Old Testament tells about the fasting journeys of several men and women. Look over the fasting stories of these biblical people to learn more about fasting: Moses (Exodus 34:27-28), the prophet Samuel (1 Samuel 7:5-6), King David (2 Samuel 12:16), the prophet Elijah (1 Kings 19:2-8), Queen Esther (Esther 4:16), and Nehemiah (Nehemiah 1:4).

When You Can't Find the Words

One of the most encouraging verses in the Bible is found in Romans 8:26–27: "In the same way, the Spirit helps us in our weakness. We do not know what we ought to pray for, but the Spirit himself intercedes for us with groans that words cannot express. And he who searches our hearts knows the mind of the Spirit, because the Spirit intercedes for the saints in accordance with God's will" (NIV). What happens when you don't feel like praying but pray anyway?

✳

When Life Overcomes You

A cynical man once said, "You are either in a crisis, coming out of a crisis, or about to go into a crisis." Jesus put it another way: "In this world you will have trouble. But take heart! I have overcome the world" (John 16:33 NIV). When life overwhelms you, you may not have the words—or the desire—to pray.

Classic commentator Matthew Henry pointed out that the word Paul used for help, *synantilambanetai*, means "The Spirit heaves with you," like a friend helping you dump a heavy load over a wall.

> GOD is in his holy Temple! Quiet everyone—a holy silence. Listen!
>
> Habakkuk 2:20 MSG
>
> Rest in the LORD and wait patiently for Him; do not fret because of him who prospers in his way, because of the man who carries out wicked schemes.
>
> Psalm 37:7 NASB

The Holy Spirit Makes Intercession

Henry said, "Why, the Spirit itself makes intercession for us, dictates our requests, indites our petitions, draws up our plea for us. Christ intercedes for us in heaven, the Spirit intercedes for us in our hearts; so graciously has God provided for the encouragement of the praying remnant. The Spirit, as an enlightening Spirit, teaches us what to pray for, as a sanctifying Spirit works and excites praying graces, as a comforting Spirit silences our fears, and helps us over all our discouragements. The Holy Spirit is the spring of all our desires and breathings towards God."

God is not uncomfortable when you fumble your prayers. He does not grow impatient as he waits on you to say what you want to say. To the contrary, God looks upon your heart and feels your prayers in the same way you do. While you struggle to put them into words, God comprehends and responds.

Points to Remember

When you feel overwhelmed, try one of these four practical activities:

• *Sing.* Find a recording of your favorite hymns or worship songs and sing along with them. Singing can focus you on the one to whom you can't pray.

• *Borrow Words.* Praying written prayers can break the dam holding back your thoughts and emotions.

• *Pray the Scriptures.* Even reading the Bible aloud can bring comfort and peace.

• *Enjoy the Silence.* Sitting quietly will let you hear God's voice more easily.

Final Thoughts

Despair and stress are not the only reasons you may find yourself without words to pray. Singer-songwriter Steven Curtis Chapman lost his voice in 2001. His career was over. Chapman said, "I didn't lose my speaking voice, which was the weird part. I thought maybe God was saying, 'I'm done with you.'" After three months, his voice miraculously returned. He was overwhelmed by God's grace.

The Lord's Prayer

It's the best-known prayer among Christians and non-Christians alike. Take a fresh look at these familiar words and glean profound insights from Jesus' model prayer.

Contents

One day Jesus was praying in a certain place.
When he finished, one of his disciples said to him,
"Lord, teach us to pray, just as John
taught his disciples."

Luke 11:1 NIV

"Our Father in Heaven"

The first rule of communication is to know your audience. Broadcasters, public speakers, pastors, and teachers all face the ongoing task of learning about their audience. In prayer, you have an audience of one. To understand your audience, it is important to understand where he lives. Heaven is a mystery that has been misunderstood and misrepresented for as long as poets and pundits have tried to define it. While it will remain mysterious until you see it with your own eyes, you can try to understand the fundamentals.

☧

God Lives in Heaven

God told Moses to create a tabernacle—a tent in which God's people could worship. Many years later, Solomon built a permanent structure, the temple, and dedicated it with a powerful prayer. Solomon acknowledged that neither a building nor the entire earth could hold God. He prayed, "Hear the humble and earnest requests from me and your people Israel when we pray toward this place. Yes, hear us from heaven where you live, and when you hear, forgive" (1 Kings 8:30 NLT).

While God dwells in heaven, he is also "close to the brokenhearted and saves those who are crushed in spirit" (Psalm 34:18 NIV). The paradox of majesty and proximity is wrapped up in the title *Father*. When you pray to the Father, you are praying to one whose wholeness cannot be contained but who is as close to you as your skin.

> Our bodies are like tents that we live in here on earth. But when these tents are destroyed, we know that God will give each of us a place to live. These homes will not be buildings that someone has made, but they are in heaven and will last forever.
>
> 2 Corinthians 5:1 CEV

> Based on His promise, we wait for new heavens and a new earth, where righteousness will dwell.
>
> 2 Peter 3:13 HCSB

Heaven Is Your Ultimate Home

Author and apologist Randy Alcorn wrote a landmark book titled *Heaven*. He wrote, "When Jesus told his disciples, 'In my Father's house are many rooms. . . . I am going there to prepare a place for you' (John 14:2), he deliberately chose common, physical terms (*house, rooms, place*) to describe where he was going and what he was preparing for us. He wanted to give his disciples (and us) something tangible to look forward to—an actual place where they (and we) would go to be with him."

Christians are ambassadors—emissaries from another country. The ambassador's permanent citizenship is in his own country. Here he is merely representing his native land on foreign soil. You are an ambassador from heaven. When you pray to God in heaven, you are sending a letter home or asking for more supplies for your outpost.

Characteristics of Heaven

Characteristic	Scripture
Eternal rewards	Matthew 5:11-12
Full of God's glory	Romans 8:16-23
Inheritance	1 Peter 1:3-4
Joyfulness	Luke 15
Peacefulness	Luke 16:19-31
Rest	Revelation 14:12-13
Righteousness	2 Peter 3:11-13
Service	Revelation 7:13-17

"Hallowed Be Your Name"

Reginald Heber wrote the lyrics for the majestic hymn "Holy, Holy, Holy." John Dykes's transforming melody made this song an enduring anthem to God's most wondrous attribute: holiness. "Holy, holy, holy! Though the darkness hide thee, though the eye of sinful man thy glory may not see; only thou art holy; there is none beside thee, perfect in power, in love, and purity." Holiness is the state of being wholly other, separate, or set apart. If God is holy, why do we pray, "Hallowed be thy *name*"?

✳

The Intent of Jesus' Words

Theologian and author R. C. Sproul pointed out that many of us miss the intent of Jesus' specific words: "The first line of the prayer is not a petition. It's a form of personal address. The prayer continues: 'hallowed be your name, your kingdom come' (Matthew 6:9-10).

"We often confuse the words 'hallowed be your name' with part of the address, as if the words were 'Hallowed is your name.' In that case the words would merely be an ascription of praise to God. But that is not how Jesus said it. He uttered it as a petition, as the first petition. We should be praying that God's name be hallowed, that God be regarded as holy."

His Son, who was born of a descendant of David according to the flesh, who was declared the Son of God with power by the resurrection from the dead, according to the Spirit of holiness, Jesus Christ our Lord.

Romans 1:3–4 NASB

He has been mindful of the humble state of his servant. From now on all generations will call me blessed, for the Mighty One has done great things for me—holy is his name. His mercy extends to those who fear him, from generation to generation.

Luke 1:48–50 NIV

The Name of God Is Holy

Sproul continued, "There is a kind of sequence within the prayer. God's kingdom will never come where His name is not considered holy. His will is not done on earth as it is in heaven if His name is desecrated here. In heaven the name of God is holy. It is breathed by angels in a sacred hush. Heaven is a place where reverence for God is total. It is foolish to look for the kingdom anywhere God is not revered."

The name for God in the Old Testament was so holy that most would not say it aloud. The scribes would not write it down. Jesus was considered blasphemous when he uttered it during his trial: "I Am." Jesus' name itself also meets the standards of holiness.

There are two types of holiness: (1) being set apart for a special purpose, and (2) set apart from evil and sin. Jesus' name meets both criteria. Jesus

was set apart for a special purpose by being named in heaven. Gabriel shocked young Mary. He told her that she would conceive and deliver a son. He instructed her to name him Jesus. Then he described what this son would become: "He will be great, and will be called the Son of the Highest; and the Lord God will give Him the throne of His father David. And He will reign over the house of Jacob forever, and of His kingdom there will be no end" (Luke 1:32–33 NKJV).

Joseph was upset. His future wife was pregnant. He thought she was pure and set apart. How could she do this to him? The angel surprised him and told him to go through with the marriage. He then said, "You shall call His name JESUS, for He will save His people from their sins" (Matthew 1:21 NKJV).

The Name of Jesus Is Set Apart

This name—*Jesus*—is set apart in history. Those who needed healing or deliverance called out the name on the street. The religious leaders cursed the name and plotted to erase it—and the man who bore the name—from the earth. His name became a part of the mocking death sentence nailed above his head on the cross: "This is Jesus, the King of the Jews."

Jesus' name is also set apart from evil and sin. It is the name Christians pray to and the name of the Savior. Paul would eventually call it the name above all names. Pastor and magazine publisher A. W. Tozer marveled at Christ's holiness: "We cannot grasp the true meaning of the divine holiness by thinking of someone or something very pure and then raising the concept to the highest degree we are capable of. God's holiness is not simply the best we know infinitely bettered. We know nothing like the divine holiness. It stands apart, unique, unapproachable, incomprehensible and unattainable. The natural man is blind to it. He may fear God's power and admire His wisdom, but His holiness he cannot even imagine." The name that we pray to is not just different or unique. It is wholly holy.

> Herod Antipas, Pontius Pilate the governor, the Gentiles, and the people of Israel were all united against Jesus, your holy servant, whom you anointed.
>
> Acts 4:27 NLT

Many names for Jesus are found in the New Testament. These names highlight the wonder and majesty of the name above all names.

New Testament Names Celebrating Jesus' Attributes and Character

Name	Scripture
Advocate	1 John 2:1
Alpha and Omega	Revelation 22:13
Author and Finisher of Our Faith	Hebrews 12:2
Bread of Life	John 6:35
Chief Cornerstone	Ephesians 2:20
Dayspring	Luke 1:78
Faithful One	Revelation 2:13
Good Shepherd	John 10:11
Guardian of Souls	1 Peter 2:25
Head of the Church	Ephesians 5:23
Holy One	Mark 1:24

New Testament Names Celebrating Jesus' Attributes and Character (cont'd)

Name	Scripture
I Am	John 8:58
Immanuel	Matthew 1:23
King of kings	1 Timothy 6:15
Lamb of God	John 1:29
Life	John 14:6
Light of the World	John 8:12
Lion of the Tribe of Judah	Revelation 5:5
Lord God Almighty	Revelation 15:3
Lord of All	Acts 10:36
Messiah	John 1:41
Morning Star	Revelation 22:16
Prince of Life	Acts 3:15
Resurrection and Life	John 11:25
Righteous Judge	2 Timothy 4:8
Root of David	Revelation 22:16
Savior	Luke 2:11
Son of God	Mark 3:11
Truth	John 14:6
Way	John 14:6
Word of Life	1 John 1:1

Something to Ponder

Jesus could've taught, "hallowed be thy character" or "thy memory." Instead, we pray, "hallowed be thy name." Songwriters Bill and Gloria Gaither created the Homecoming concert series where the audience sings along with well-known recording artists. The chorus "There's Just Something About That Name" is one of the highlights. The lyrics and emotion underline the nature of the name of Jesus. His name should be spoken in reverence, never as a punctuation mark or expletive.

"Your Kingdom Come"

Many of Jesus' parables begin with the words "The kingdom of God is like . . ." His descriptions are like snapshots of remote Australia or the moon tacked upon a bulletin board. The more you look at them, the more you want to see the entirety of the landscape and experience it for yourself. When the kingdom of God is fully realized, all pain, suffering, mourning, and tears will evaporate faster than the morning dew. Theologians call this the second advent. As Israel looked forward to the coming of the Messiah, so Christians long for the coming of the kingdom of God.

☧

The Kingdom of God Is Full of Mysteries

The disciples questioned Jesus often about his parables. They were looking at his snapshots but not understanding the panoramic picture. Jesus told them, "The secret of the kingdom of God has been given to you" (Mark 4:11 NIV). The disciples still struggled with the meanings of Jesus' teaching. Jesus was pointing to himself as the fulfillment of the prophecies and the personification of the kingdom of God. Yet the disciples were still searching for—like many of their contemporaries—a political coup d'état.

[Jesus] entered the synagogue and continued speaking out boldly for three months, reasoning and persuading them about the kingdom of God.

Acts 19:8 NASB

The kingdom of God is not eating and drinking, but righteousness, peace, and joy in the Holy Spirit.

Romans 14:17 HCSB

The Kingdom of God Is Not of This World

Jesus did not come to overthrow earthly kingdoms or unseat military dictators. During his trial, Pilate questioned him about his identity and mission. Jesus answered, "My kingdom is not of this world. If My kingdom were of this world, My servants would fight, so that I should not be delivered to the Jews; but now My kingdom is not from here" (John 18:36 NKJV).

In his longest teaching session—often referred to as the Sermon on the Mount—Jesus urged his followers to "seek first His kingdom and His righteousness" (Matthew 6:33 NASB) but didn't promise that they would fully realize it until he comes again.

When the apostle John described the second advent, his words were still full of mystery and surprise: "I saw the holy city, the new Jerusalem, coming down from God out of heaven like a bride beautifully dressed for her husband. I heard a loud shout from the throne, saying, 'Look, God's home is now among his people! He will live with them, and they will be his people. God himself will be with them'" (Revelation 21:2-3 NLT).

The Kingdom of God Is Within You

The paradox of proximity exists with the presence of God—he is both infinitely above you and intimately close to you. The same paradox exists with the kingdom of God. It is not of this world and is simultaneously within you. This paradox should inspire awe and tenderness.

Fifteenth-century Catholic monk Thomas à Kempis challenged himself and his readers to "turn, then, to God with all your heart. Forsake this wretched world and your soul shall find rest." To Thomas, the kingdom of God—the gifts of peace and joy that only the Holy Spirit can give—belong exclusively to those who have learned to "despise" the external things of the world and embrace instead the inner, communal life with God.

He urged his readers to prepare a dwelling place for Christ in their hearts, a place that delights the Lord and welcomes his comfort and presence: "His visits with the inward man are frequent, His communion sweet and full of consolation, His peace great, and His intimacy wonderful indeed."

Christ Has Already Won the War

The Bible shows us the end of the story—the Enemy of your soul is eternally defeated—but there are days when you feel like the war will never end.

> The Kingdom of God is not just a lot of talk; it is living by God's power.
>
> 1 Corinthians 4:20 NLT

Dutch-born seminary professor Anthony Hoekema compared the now-and-not-yet of God's kingdom to the end of World War II. "Suppose that up in the almost inaccessible north some small village with a Nazi overlord failed to hear the news of the liberation for some weeks. During that time, we might put it, the inhabitants of the village were living in the 'old' time of Nazi occupation instead of the 'new' time of Norwegian liberation."

When you pray for God's kingdom to come, you are praying under occupation for the coming liberation. To put it another way, you are like a citizen of a medieval city; when trouble comes, you run across the drawbridge into the safety of the walls and allow the Lord to defend you with the vast resources of his kingdom. When you pray for God's kingdom to come, you acknowledge his power and victory.

Final Thoughts

Consider the thieves crucified on either side of Jesus. They represent the tension between the kingdom of this world and the kingdom of God. They both mocked him, but one wised up and said to Jesus, "'Remember me when you come into power!' Jesus replied, 'I promise that today you will be with me in paradise'" (Luke  23:42-43 CEV). When you pray "Your kingdom come," hear Jesus' response: "You will be with me in paradise."

The Kingdom of God

Scripture	Description
Matthew 6:10	Should be prayed for
Matthew 3:2; Mark 1:15	Is near
Matthew 6:33	Should be sought
Matthew 13:24–30	Is like a farmer
Matthew 13:31–32	Is like a mustard seed
Matthew 13:47–50	Is like a net
Matthew 19:23–24	Is difficult to enter
Matthew 20:1–16	Is like a landowner
Matthew 22:2–14	Is like a king
Luke 17:21	Is within you
Luke 18:17	Is for childlike faith
Luke 18:29–30	Should be primary
John 3:1–8	Is for the born again
John 18:36	Is not of this world
Romans 14:17	Is spiritual
Ephesians 5:5	Is pure
Colossians 1:13	Is full of light
Hebrews 1:8; 2 Peter 1:11; Revelation 11:15	Will last forever
Revelation 5:9	Is universal
Revelation 5:13–14	Is omnipresent

"Your Will Be Done on Earth as It Is in Heaven"

Amazon.com lists more than twenty-five thousand books written about how to discover God's will for your life. Christians throughout time have been frustrated trying to find the secret code or formula. *A + B* doesn't equal *C.* Jesus prayed for God's will. He also told believers that he will grant whatever is prayed according to God's will. If God's will is so important to the Christian faith, why does it feel so elusive?

Imagine yourself as the apprentice to a master painter such as Rembrandt. What if instead of applying the paint to the canvas himself, he talked you through every brushstroke in an attempt to paint his vision through your hands? How well would you do?

> Do not be foolish, but understand what the Lord's will is.
>
> Ephesians 5:17 NIV
>
> It is better, if it is God's will, to suffer for doing good than for doing evil.
>
> 1 Peter 3:17 NIV

God's Will

God has chosen to coach us through accomplishing his will. He teaches us about his will through the examples of the heroes and heroines of the Bible. They are his masterworks.

If you travel to Paris or Rome, you'll see art students of every age and ability copying the work of the masters. They sit for hours in front of a painting at a museum to try to capture and understand what the artist was trying to accomplish. Some art students have sketchbooks full of hands as rendered by their favorite artists. They hope to capture the nuance of his or her work. In the same way, you must become a student of the will of God and sit for hours watching the lives of the men and women of the Bible.

Heroes and Heroines

Here are some questions to consider as you study the lives of Bible heroes and heroines:

- How did he handle adversity?

- How did she respond to failure?

- How did God speak to him?

- Who was her archenemy?

- How did the Enemy attempt to derail him?

- How did she complain?

- How did he worship?

When you pray for God's will, you join Jesus in his prayers. At his darkest hour, he prayed, "Not My will, but Yours be done" (Luke 22:42 NASB).

Something to Ponder

The most important aspect of pursuing the will of God is attitude. Micah 6:8 tells us that walking humbly with God is incredibly important. When frustration grows but you don't understand the will of God, pull back, take a deep breath, and remember to humble yourself before him. Ask him to show you his will.

Final Thoughts

Think about a bottle of kids' soap bubbles. When you pull out the wand, it drips with the thick, glistening liquid, but there are no bubbles until you gently blow behind the ring. Each day is like a ring of soap bubbles. Like the original creation, you must await the breath of God. Only then can you soar. Pray for his will to be done, and get ready to fly.

"Give Us This Day Our Daily Bread"

When the disciples heard Jesus ask for daily bread, they probably thought back on the familiar history of the exodus. While the Israelites wandered through the wilderness, God miraculously met their physical needs with a daily shower of manna. Manna was waferlike pieces of sweet bread that covered the ground every morning like fresh snow. Even though God gave them more than enough for each day, the extra couldn't be saved. God generously fed them constantly and consistently, but the people grumbled against his provision. Did Jesus want them to pray for manna again, or did he mean something else?

✳

Another Miracle with Bread

A few weeks after Jesus taught his disciples how to pray, he performed another bread miracle: the feeding of five thousand men plus wives and children in one day. There may have been more than twenty thousand people fed on that single day. Jesus miraculously transformed five small loaves and two fish into a smorgasbord for a crowd that would overflow a high school football stadium. That puts a twist in the equation—what is daily bread?

Bread is what you need—physically, intellectually, emotionally, relationally, and spiritually. Pray for the necessities, not the niceties of life. It's too easy to be distracted from what's important.

"The bread of God is that which comes down out of heaven, and gives life to the world." Then they said to Him, "Lord, always give us this bread." Jesus said to them, "I am the bread of life; he who comes to Me will not hunger, and he who believes in Me will never thirst."

John 6:33–35 NASB

Teach us to number our days carefully so that we may develop wisdom in our hearts.

Psalm 90:12 HCSB

During the Korean War, a general commissioned his staff to survey all his commanding officers about their most acute needs. His staff visited with COs leading infantry units at the front, managing M*A*S*H* units a few miles back, and supervising headquarters staff. The results startled the general. Those at the front lines asked for more ammunition, more bandages, and more soldiers. Those farthest away from the fighting asked for Coca-Cola and better movies. The general reminded everyone that they were fighting a war, not taking a vacation.

You are on the front lines, not the sidelines, of your life. When you pray, avoid the temptation to pray for daily cupcakes. Allow God to supply your needs and bless you beyond belief.

Day by Day

Someone once quipped, "Life wouldn't be so hard if it wasn't so daily." The movie *Groundhog Day* hits home because viewers feel trapped in

the monotony of the daily grind. A few minutes after Jesus taught the model prayer, he coached his disciples on worry. He said, "Do not worry about tomorrow; for tomorrow will care for itself. Each day has enough trouble of its own" (Matthew 6:34 NASB).

When you pray for daily bread, ask God for what you will need for the next twenty-four hours. Prisoners of war have reported praying hour-by-hour or minute-by-minute.

Consider the Lilies

It's as if Jesus anticipated our problems with praying for his will and for daily bread. Almost in the same breath as his instructions on prayer, Jesus said, "Look at the ravens. They don't plant or harvest or store food in barns, for God feeds them. And you are far more valuable to him than any birds! Can all your worries add a single moment to your life? And if worry can't accomplish a little thing like that, what's the use of worrying over bigger things? Look at the lilies and how they grow. They don't work or make their clothing, yet Solomon in all his glory was not dressed as beautifully as they are" (Luke 12:24–27 NLT).

When you doubt his provision and pray for daily bread with a skeptical heart, look around at the majesty of creation that he holds together.

Jesus Is the Bread of Life

After Jesus fed the multitudes, the crowd became too rowdy. Jesus headed to the mountains, and the disciples headed to the water. A storm tossed the ship in the middle of the night. While they trimmed sails, they spotted Jesus walking across the lake. They invited him into the boat and "immediately the boat was at the land to which they were going" (John 6:21 NASB). The crowds chased Jesus all the way to Capernaum. They were hunting for more food and more miracles.

> How do you know what your life will be like tomorrow? Your life is like the morning fog—it's here a little while, then it's gone.
>
> James 4:14 NLT

Jesus excited them when he said, "The bread of God is that which comes down out of heaven, and gives life to the world" (John 6:33 NASB).

The crowd only cheered for more, but he silenced them. "I am the bread of life; he who comes to Me will not hunger, and he who believes in Me will never thirst" (John 6:35 NASB). When you pray for daily bread, don't forget that the ultimate bread is Jesus himself. Ask him to draw close, to surprise you amid your stormy seas, and to be the provision that never leaves you hungry.

Point to Remember

Goal-setters struggle with the concept of daily bread. "Isn't it wise to think ahead?" they argue. "Doesn't the Bible say, 'Count the cost'?" It does, but the Bible also warns, "The mind of man plans his way, but the LORD directs his steps" (Proverbs 16:9 NASB). Ask God for today's dose of planning ahead, always remembering that he clothes every bird and flower.

Digging Deeper

All the requests in the Lord's Prayer—including daily bread—are plural. Bible scholar Hank Hanegraaff observed, "Not only are we praying for the needs of our immediate family, but we are praying for the needs of our extended family as well. We do not pray as mere rugged individualists but as members of a community of faith. All we need to do is turn on the television to see that our sisters and brothers around the world suffer daily from maladies ranging from droughts to deadly diseases. Yet, these images fade from our minds before the next commercial interruption."

Final Thoughts

Agur, son of Jakeh, compiled the wise sayings for what is now known as Proverbs 30. He asked for daily bread in his wise prayer. "Keep falsehood and lies far from me; give me neither poverty nor riches, but give me only my daily bread. Otherwise, I may have too much and disown you and say, 'Who is the Lord?' Or I may become poor and steal, and so dishonor the name of my God" (30:8-9 NIV).

"Forgive Us Our Debts, as We Forgive Our Debtors"

Have you been in a church service or meeting where everyone joins in praying the Lord's Prayer aloud? If many backgrounds are represented, this phrase will bring chaos—and a few smiles—to the assembly. Do you use the word *debts* or *trespasses*? No matter which word you use, this phrase is special. The fifth commandment is the first with a promise, and the fifth request in the Lord's Prayer is the first with an elaboration.

✳

Jesus used the Greek word *opheilema*: "a debt that is due today." Like the request before it, there is immediacy to this phrase—debts are current. Immediately after teaching the prayer, Jesus said, "If you forgive others for their transgressions, your heavenly Father will also forgive you. But if you do not forgive others, then your Father will not forgive your transgressions" (Matthew 6:14–15 NASB).

An Unforgiving Heart

This is not a heavenly quid pro quo. Jesus was illustrating the insidious nature of an unforgiving heart. He told his followers two parables. First, a wealthy man forgave two debts. The first debtor owed two years of wages; the second owed two months. Jesus asked, "Which of them will love the wealthy man more?" They answered, "The one forgiven more."

> Be kind and compassionate to one another, forgiving one another, just as God also forgave you in Christ.
>
> Ephesians 4:32 HCSB

> If we claim to be without sin, we deceive ourselves and the truth is not in us. If we confess our sins, he is faithful and just and will forgive us our sins and purify us from all unrighteousness. If we claim we have not sinned, we make him out to be a liar and his word has no place in our lives.
>
> 1 John 1:8–10 NIV

He also told a parable about a man who was forgiven for millions in debt but then turned around and refused to forgive a man for a tiny debt.

An Unforgiving Spirit

Pastor and author John Piper wrote, "If we hold fast to an unforgiving spirit, we will lose heaven, and gain hell. The reason is not because we can earn heaven or merit heaven by forgiving others, but because holding fast to an unforgiving spirit proves that we do not trust Christ. If we trust him, we will not be able to take forgiveness from his hand for our million-dollar debt and withhold it from our ten dollar debtor."

When you pray, "Forgive us our debts," remind yourself of the inestimable value of his forgiveness.

Digging Deeper

 A Pharisee invited Jesus to dinner. As they dined, a woman burst into the room. She knelt at Jesus' feet and sparked incredulity and insolence from the religious leaders. Her tears dripped onto Jesus' feet. She wiped them with her hair and then poured an expensive oil onto them, anointing Jesus. Jesus told the table of slack-jawed men, "Her many sins have been forgiven—for she loved much. But he who has been forgiven little loves little" (Luke 7:47 NIV).

Check Your Understanding

- **What is forgiveness of sin?**

To forgive sin is to take away iniquity. It is a metaphor. A man carries a heavy burden, and another man comes and lifts it off. When the heavy burden of sin is on us, God in pardoning lifts it off from the conscience, and lays it upon Christ.

"Do Not Lead Us into Temptation, but Deliver Us from the Evil One"

Some have joked that this entreaty is the most often prayed phrase of the Lord's Prayer. Temptations seem to be around every corner. What tempts you? The bowl of chocolate candies on a coworker's desk? Clicking on the wrong link while surfing the Internet? Expanding a simple misunderstanding into an outright lie? Spending money reserved for another part of the budget? Jesus was tempted but withstood the onslaught on your behalf. His model prayer can encourage and strengthen you.

✵

Temptation

The phrase "Do not lead us into temptation" should not be expanded to say, "Sometimes you do lead us into temptation; don't do it anymore." Pastor and author John MacArthur pointed out that this "petition reflects the believing one's desire to avoid the dangers of sin altogether."

> Return, O Lord, and rescue me. Save me because of your unfailing love.
>
> Psalm 6:4 NLT
>
> Watch and pray so that you will not fall into temptation. The spirit is willing, but the body is weak.
>
> Matthew 26:41 NIV

James watched Jesus travel around Nazareth, Bethany, and other towns in Judea. He was part of the family mob that showed up at Peter's house for an intervention (Mark 3). He faced the most cunning and destructive temptation of all—disbelieving Jesus. But as Jesus' ministry continued, James came to embrace Jesus' teachings and became a leader in the early church. He saw Jesus flee from and avoid temptation. He was up close and personal.

James wrote in his epistle, "Let no one say when he is tempted, 'I am being tempted by God'; for God cannot be tempted by evil, and He

Himself does not tempt anyone" (James 1:13 NASB). The Devil must love to tempt a believer to believe his tempter is God himself.

The apostle Paul had something in common with James: he disbelieved Jesus until God got his attention on the road to Damascus (Acts 9). He offered this warning and promise: "Whoever thinks he stands must be careful not to fall! No temptation has overtaken you except what is common to humanity. God is faithful and He will not allow you to be tempted beyond what you are able, but with the temptation He will also provide a way of escape, so that you are able to bear it" (1 Corinthians 10:12–13 HCSB).

God knows the way of escape and will deliver you.

The Evil One

Part of military basic training takes place in the classroom. New soldiers learn the uniform colors, insignia, silhouettes of aircraft and tanks, and the weapons used by their enemies. In the same way, Christians should understand the profile of their Enemy.

The Bible calls the Devil arrogant and rash. The apostle Peter, who denied Christ three times, understood the nature of the Devil. In his letter, Peter wrote, "Be sober, be vigilant; because your adversary the devil walks about like a roaring lion, seeking whom he may devour" (1 Peter 5:8 NKJV).

The Bible also calls the Devil crafty and deceitful. Paul often pointed to how Satan tempted Eve as an example of how he twists words. The psalmist compared Satan to a hunter: "Surely He shall deliver you from the snare of the fowler" (Psalm 91:3 NKJV). Jesus referred to him as a wolf in one of his parables (John 10:12).

"Bible Answer Man" Hank Hanegraaff warned Christians of the dangers of either overestimating or underestimating Satan's power.

He took issue with those who describe Satan using terms such as the "author of darkness"; in so doing, he said, they unwittingly draw a parallel between him and God, the Author of light. He wrote, "That, however, is far from true. God is the sovereign Author of all creation; Satan is but an angel that he has created. Satan is not the opposite of the Creator. Rather, as a fallen angel, he is the counterpart to the archangel Michael."

But underestimating Satan is also a mistake, he wrote, reminding readers that though he is malevolent, Satan also possesses a brilliant intellect. Hanegraaff quotes Charles Haddon Spurgeon: "We must not expect that a man, unaided from above, should ever be a match for an angel, especially an angel whose intellect has been sharpened by malice."

> Consider it pure joy, my brothers, whenever you face trials of many kinds, because you know that the testing of your faith develops perseverance.
>
> James 1:2–3 NIV

When you pray "Deliver us from evil," pray with confidence and courage that God will answer and deliver.

Check Your Understanding

- **Will Satan be defeated? If so, when?**

Think of Satan as a bull in a nineteenth-century bullfight. As you interact with him on earth, remember that he is stabbed, bleeding, and near death. He is still dangerous, but already defeated. He is crushed (Genesis 3:15), and it's only a matter of time until he is destroyed (Revelation 20:14).

- **How should a person behave when tempted?**

You should first prepare yourself for temptation. It will come. It is foolish to believe you are immune (Ephesians 6:11). When temptation comes, take your cue from Joseph. When Potiphar's wife tried to seduce him, Joseph immediately escaped and ran so fast that his tunic remained in her hand (Genesis 39).

- If a person has given in to temptation repeatedly, how can he possibly pray this prayer?

The apostle Paul called himself the chief of sinners, yet knew great mercy and grace. God's grace is for you as well. Receive it and be refreshed (1 Timothy 1).

Final Thoughts

Hank Hanegraaff said: "It is significant to note that Jesus was led *by the Spirit* into the desert 'to be tempted by the devil' (Matthew 4:1). Thus while Satan was the *agent of the temptation*, God was the *author of the testing*. Satan used the occasion to tempt Christ to sin; God used the occasion to demonstrate that he could not sin."

Something to Ponder

Some Christians who are dealing with temptation tend to focus on the sin rather than the cure. While it's important to acknowledge the specific sin you're battling, obsessing over it—or worrying about whether that sin is worse than others—won't help you conquer it. Once you confess the sin to God and resolve to turn away from it, it's time to focus on God and the power he gives you to overcome sin.

"For Yours Is the Kingdom and the Power and the Glory Forever"

The ending to the Lord's Prayer is controversial, and it does not appear in some of the manuscripts of the gospel of Matthew. In many Bibles, footnotes mark this fact. Biblical scholars fill in the details from history. The words echo 1 Chronicles 29:11, a psalm of thanksgiving written by David in response to the outpouring of offerings for the construction of the temple. The words became the response of God's people in the synagogue. After a prayer was offered, the people would respond, "For yours is the kingdom and the power and the glory forever." Christians carry on the tradition even today.

✳

Praise God

Bible commentator Matthew Henry highlighted this verse. The temple was built for the glory of God, David's psalm points to the worship of God, and those who say these words are intended to be conduits of praise to God. Praise is integral to prayer. The model prayer begins by ascribing praise to God. It is appropriate that the disciples would respond with the words of praise they had been taught since childhood.

When you praise God, you magnify him. When Mary, the mother of Jesus, discovered God's plan, she said, "My soul magnifies the Lord." Sherlock Holmes magnified clues with his magnifying glass, and scientists magnify cells with a microscope.

> In love he predestined us to be adopted as his sons through Jesus Christ, in accordance with his pleasure and will—to the praise of his glorious grace, which he has freely given us in the One he loves.
>
> Ephesians 1:4–6 NIV

Magnify God

When you magnify God, you are not a microscope; you don't make the very small a little larger. Instead, you are like a telescope that magnifies a celestial object hundreds of light-years away and larger than our entire solar system. The naked eye can see it, but magnification sharpens the details and inspires more awe of its beauty.

God is larger than you can imagine, and your praise brings the details of his majesty into clearer focus and stirs your heart to even more worship. In prayer, step up to the telescope and become amazed with God. Don't sit on the couch and let others look through the lens.

Why We Praise God

His Attributes	His Actions
Excellent (Exodus 15:7)	Consolation (Isaiah 12:1)
Faithful (Isaiah 25:1)	Counsel (Jeremiah 32:19)
Full of glory (Ezekiel 3:12)	Deliverance (Psalm 40:1-3)
Good (Jeremiah 33:11)	Forgiveness (Hosea 14:2)
Great (1 Chronicles 16:25)	Justice (Psalm 101:1)
Holy (Isaiah 6:3)	Promises (1 Kings 8:56)
Hope of glory (1 Peter 1:3-4)	Protection (Psalm 59:17)
Majestic (Psalm 96:2-6)	Salvation (Luke 1:68-69)
Merciful (2 Chronicles 20:21)	Works (Psalm 150)
Powerful (Psalm 21:13)	
Truthful (Psalm 138:2)	
Wise (Jude 25)	

Great Prayers of History

From medieval Europe to twentieth-century America come some of the most memorable prayers in the history of the Christian faith. Following are seven that have inspired millions of people over the years.

Contents

Whenever we are in need, we should come bravely
before the throne of our merciful God. There we
will be treated with undeserved kindness,
and we will find help.

Hebrews 4:16 CEV

The Serenity Prayer—Praying for Wisdom

The Lord's Prayer is the most frequently prayed prayer in history. Second place is awarded to the Serenity Prayer. Soldiers in Europe and the Pacific during World War II heard their chaplains pray it. Now, every day, millions worldwide pray the Serenity Prayer to begin group meetings as they seek healing and restoration. The prayer appears on every surface from framed fine art and building-size murals to snow globes and ink pens. The prayer's popularity is exceeded only by its wisdom.

⁑

Reinhold Niebuhr was born at the turn of the twentieth century just as the industrial revolution was picking up steam. After graduation from Yale in 1914, he was assigned to a church in Detroit, Michigan. His church grew quickly because of his winsome preaching and the burgeoning automobile industry. In 1928, Niebuhr joined the faculty of Union Theological Seminary in New York. His teaching and writing influenced generations of students, including Dietrich Bonhoeffer, the great German writer and theologian.

Niebuhr composed the prayer while preaching in Heath, Massachusetts, while his family was on vacation. His daughter wrote, "It was in an ordinary Sunday morning service at the Heath Union Church in the summer of 1943 that my father first used his new prayer."

> May the God of hope fill you with all joy and peace as you trust in him, so that you may overflow with hope by the power of the Holy Spirit.
>
> Romans 15:13 NIV
>
> God has not given us a spirit of fear and timidity, but of power, love, and self-discipline.
>
> 2 Timothy 1:7 NLT

The original version of the prayer for wisdom reads, "God, give us grace to accept with serenity the things that cannot be changed, courage to change the things that should be changed, and the wisdom to distinguish the one from the other." Three requests are wrapped up in these famous words.

Serenity

Peace feels fleeting. To-do lists are long and complicated by overcommitment. Interruptions add insult to injury. Visual stimuli come from LCD screens on phones, computers, televisions, and even billboards. Noises bombard our ears from every direction and source. One day ends in frustration, and another day begins owing debts to yesterday. It seems impossible to find a moment for a deep breath and a free thought.

God offers a different peace. As Jesus prepared his disciples for his death, he told them, "Peace I leave with you; my peace I give you. I do not give to you as the world gives. Do not let your hearts be troubled and do not be afraid" (John 14:27 NIV). His peace is better than a soothing bath and can permeate the most difficult schedule.

Courage

Paul began each of his letters by bestowing God's grace on the readers. He ended every letter with a flurry of instructions. Some are common and others pointed. At the end of his first letter to the church at Corinth, Paul admonished the leaders, "Watch, stand fast in the faith, be brave, be strong. Let all that you do be done with love" (1 Corinthians 16:13–14 NKJV). The Corinthians didn't need courage to fight a battle or hold off a siege, they needed courage to confront false ideas about faith, old habits of idolatry, and a hedonistic culture.

God's courage has more steel in it than earthly courage. His courage is reinforced by his omnipotence—his all-powerful nature. When you pray for courage, remember that God encouraged Joshua, David, and Jeremiah, and the persecuted church before you.

Wisdom

Niebuhr's ultimate prayer is for wisdom. Solomon, often called the wisest man who ever lived, discussed the value of wisdom in Proverbs 4:5-9, advising his "son" to actively pursue wisdom. Wisdom, it seems, is not something that comes to people automatically, and it is something that people can forget. Not only did Solomon warn against forgetting wisdom; he also warned against abandoning it. Wisdom (which he personified in female terms) will guard over those who cling to her, he wrote, and those who place great value on her will be exalted.

> The fear of the LORD is the beginning of knowledge; fools despise wisdom and instruction.
>
> Proverbs 1:7 NASB

By asking for wisdom, Niebuhr echoed the observation of James that those who lacked wisdom could ask God to supply it. God, in his generosity of spirit, would grant that request "without reproach" (James 1:5 NASB)—without expressing any disapproval over that lack of wisdom. Solomon, James, and Reinhold Niebuhr—three men who believed God's promise to give his people wisdom. That promise is for you as well.

Myth Buster

Some say that Reinhold Niebuhr didn't really write the Serenity Prayer, and the answer is a bit uncertain. In 2008, Fred Shapiro, the editor of *The Yale Book of Quotations*, asserted that the prayer was in circulation at least six years before it was attributed to the pastor. Niebuhr himself was modest about his composition.  He said, "Of course, it may have been spooking around for years, even centuries, but I don't think so. I honestly do believe that I wrote it myself." The prayer now reads: "God grant me the serenity to accept the things I cannot change, courage to change the things I can, and wisdom to know the difference."

Something to Ponder

Alcoholics Anonymous added another section to the prayer: "Living one day at a time; enjoying one moment at a time; accepting hardships as the pathway to peace; taking, as He did, this sinful world as it is, not as I would have it; trusting that He will make all things right if I surrender to His Will; so that I may be reasonably happy in this life and supremely happy with Him forever and ever in the next."

Final Thoughts

Solomon was given the opportunity to receive unequaled wealth or unparalleled wisdom from God. He chose wisdom, and God bestowed riches, wisdom, and honor. God then encouraged Solomon with these words: "If you walk in My ways, to keep My statutes and my commandments, as your father David walked, then I will lengthen your days" (1 Kings 3:14 NKJV). May God grant you wisdom—and much more.

Check Your Understanding

- **How does acceptance result in serenity?**

Implied in the Serenity Prayer is the concept of relinquishment; in accepting that you cannot change a situation, you relinquish your attempt to control the situation. And with that comes peace.

- **How can a person acquire courage?**

The Bible tells of many people who lacked courage but became bold by God's power. Each Spirit-led courageous act emboldens preparation for the next one.

The Prayer of Saint Francis of Assisi—Praying for Peace

Francesco felt caught between his parents. His mother wanted him to grow up to be a great spiritual leader. His father, a fabric salesman, wanted his son to grow up in the family business. Francesco made his own path by becoming a troubadour and poet. After a while, however, he saw the wisdom of his mom's ideas. Francesco—or Francis as he would be known in English—decided to dedicate his life to simplicity, devotion, and living out the love of Christ.

Instrument of Peace

Saint Francis founded the Franciscan order of monks but is ultimately best known for his poetic prayer:

"Lord, make me an instrument of Thy peace; where there is hatred, let me sow love; where there is injury, pardon; where there is doubt, faith; where there is despair, hope; where there is darkness, light; and where there is sadness, joy. O Divine Master, grant that I may not so much seek to be consoled as to console; to be understood, as to understand; to be loved, as to love; for it is in giving that we receive, it is in pardoning that we are pardoned, and it is in dying that we are born to Eternal Life. Amen."

His words gather together scriptural admonitions like so many roses in a

Blessed be the God and Father of our Lord Jesus Christ, the Father of mercies and God of all comfort, who comforts us in all our affliction so that we will be able to comfort those who are in any affliction with the comfort with which we ourselves are comforted by God.

2 Corinthians 1:3–4 NASB

I have been a constant example of how you can help those in need by working hard. You should remember the words of the Lord Jesus: "It is more blessed to give than to receive."

Acts 20:35 NLT

bouquet. His requests reflect the "fruit of the Spirit" (Galatians 5:22–23) and "the Beatitudes" (Matthew 5). Early in his life, Saint Francis was known as a flashy dresser who liked to pick a fight, spend a franc, and woo women. His narcissism gave way to humility, however, when he saw genuine poverty and need. This prayer is offered out of that humility.

Inspiration of Generations

The simplicity of his poetry belies his troubadour spirit and shines a spotlight on a code of behavior. This prayer has inspired three generations of songwriters, painters, and pastors to hone their crafts, at the same time motivating missionaries and caregivers to serve another day.

Myth Buster

Did Saint Francis really write this prayer? Scholars are divided. The prayer as it appears in English can be traced back only to 1936 when copies were distributed during World War II. A similar prayer appeared in a French Catholic journal, *La Clochette* ("The Little Bell"), in 1912 and became wildly popular when published in the official papal newspaper, *Osservatore Romano*. The prayer may not be from the thirteenth century, but it does reflect the ideals of Saint Francis.

Something to Ponder

Rich Mullins wrote songs like "Awesome God" and "Elijah." He was fascinated by Saint Francis after seeing *Brother Sun, Sister Moon*, a biography directed by Franco Zefferelli. Mullins said, "That's really what I want to do. I mean, I really do want to live in poverty, I really do want my life to mean something. I really do want to imitate Christ and live according to the rule of the gospels."

Saint Patrick's Prayer—
Praying for God's Protection

Few people in church history have as many legends attached to them as does Saint Patrick. He lived in the fifth century, and few verifiable records of his life survive from that time. The fifteen hundred years since then provided plenty of time and opportunities for stories to be handed down—and to grow to mythic proportions. One story about him is unquestionably true, however, and it's a good one: Saint Patrick expanded the presence of Christianity in Ireland, and things were never quite the same after that.

✳

Most of what is known about Patrick can be traced to two surviving letters, one of which told the story of his life. Much of what he wrote rings true to historians and lines up with what is known about the British Isles during that period.

Faith in Christ

Here is what is believed to be true: Patrick was born in Britain to a wealthy Roman family—his father was a not-particularly-religious Christian deacon—toward the end of the fourth century. At the age of sixteen, Patrick was sold into slavery by Irish kidnappers. During captivity, his faith in Christ was sealed and began to grow. Six years later—by his account, in obedience to the voice of God—he escaped and returned to his family. Soon thereafter he left for France to prepare for the priesthood. All along, his intention was to spread the gospel of Christ to the Irish.

Go into all the world and preach the gospel to every creature. He who believes and is baptized will be saved; but he who does not believe will be condemned.

Mark 16:15–16 NKJV

If any of you wants to be my follower, you must turn from your selfish ways, take up your cross daily, and follow me.

Luke 9:23 NLT

When he returned to Ireland, he faced significant opposition from the Druids, a religious order who worshipped nature and didn't appreciate the presence of Christians. As Patrick and his followers traveled through the countryside on their way to meet with the king, a group of Druids lay in wait. Patrick learned of the planned ambush and wrote a prayer for protection that he placed on his breastplate. The prayer has come to be known as the Lorica, or the Deer's Cry; as Patrick and his twenty men passed by the Druids, all the would-be attackers saw were a doe and twenty fawns.

Saint Patrick's Prayer

These are the best-known, and most frequently prayed, words from Patrick's prayer: "Christ be with me, Christ within me, / Christ behind me, Christ before me, / Christ beside me, Christ to win me, / Christ to comfort and restore me, / Christ beneath me, Christ above me, / Christ in quiet, Christ in danger, / Christ in hearts of all that love me, / Christ in mouth of friend and stranger."

Patrick went on to tirelessly evangelize the people of Ireland. According to his autobiographical letter, he baptized thousands of people, ordained  priests, founded a number of monasteries, established church councils and dioceses, and led wealthy women and princes to Christ. Some of the women became nuns, which didn't sit well with their families.

Some of Patrick's evangelistic methods were highly criticized at the time, but many became patterns for sharing Christ that survive to this day. He was the first Christian to undertake a massive evangelistic effort, proving that believers did not need special training or advanced education to preach the gospel and make disciples of all nations.

Rituals and Symbols

Patrick also took a cue from the apostle Paul, who used elements of pagan culture to explain Christianity (Acts 17). He is credited with using rituals and symbols used by the Irish in their nature worship. The familiar Celtic cross was Patrick's creation; he believed that incorporating the sun with the cross of Christ would help the Irish—who worshipped the sun—understand that Jesus was to be worshipped. And instead of trying to do away with the god-honoring bonfires the Irish were accustomed to, Patrick began using them during Easter services.

> The harvest is plentiful but the workers are few. Ask the Lord of the harvest, therefore, to send out workers into his harvest field.
>
> Matthew 9:37–38 NIV

His efforts served one purpose, to bring glory and honor to Christ. The changed lives of the Irish people were a testament to that; Patrick placed as much emphasis on a life of holiness as he did on salvation, and he made disciples of new believers to follow his lead.

Patrick is believed to have died in the year 461 on March 17—known today as Saint Patrick's Day, the date set aside by the Roman Catholic Church to honor him. In Ireland, the day is also set aside for prayers on behalf of worldwide missionaries—a fitting tribute to the country's best-known evangelist.

Myth Buster

Of all the legends about Patrick's life, the best-known credits the saint with ridding Ireland of snakes. The stories vary, but the most common one has Patrick using a wooden staff to drive the snakes into the sea. There's just one problem: there were no snakes in Ireland at the time. Any snakes that may have lived there would  have been buried by deep sheets of glacial ice during the Pleistocene period. By the time the ice melted, Ireland was separated from the nearest landmass by twelve miles. Snakes cannot travel that far in water.

Further Insights

Saint Patrick influenced future missions in two other ways:

- Although he came from wealth, Patrick renounced his background and lived among the poor Irish as they did, believing that they would be more inclined to listen to his message about Christ if he shared their way of living.

- Because he had little education, Patrick had difficulty communicating with those who spoke different languages. His openness in describing the challenges he faced prompted future foreign missionaries to begin learning the required languages before leaving for the mission field.

Digging Deeper

Acts 17:22–29 records the apostle Paul's method for preaching Christ to pagans in Athens. Standing before a crowd of Athenians, Paul commended them for taking their religion seriously. "I even found an altar with this inscription: TO AN UNKNOWN GOD. Now what you worship as something unknown I am going to proclaim to you," Paul told the crowd (v. 23 NIV). He then proceeded to inform the Athenians about this "unknown god"—the Creator God who is so powerful and mighty that he cannot be contained by shrines—unlike the gods the Greeks worshipped.

Abraham Lincoln's Proclamation—
Praying for Forgiveness

Though he is occasionally edged out by George Washington in presidential popularity polls, Abraham Lincoln is the U.S. president most often cited as the "most influential" or "most highly regarded." His wit and humility made him a man of the people, while his wisdom steered the country through one of the most difficult times in its history. In Lincoln's own words, it was prayer that saw him through: "I have been driven many times to my knees by the overwhelming conviction that I had nowhere else to go."

✺

Prayer and Humiliation

Given his well-documented dependence on prayer, it's not surprising that Abraham Lincoln set aside a national day of "prayer and humiliation" in the spring of 1863, two years into the Civil War.

The proclamation suggested that the Civil War was God's punishment for the country's sins and a call to national reformation. After listing the many blessings of God on the United States, Lincoln wrote: "Intoxicated with unbroken success, we have become too self-sufficient to feel the necessity of redeeming and preserving grace, too proud to pray to the God that made us! It behooves us then, to humble ourselves before the offended Power, to confess our national sins, and to pray for clemency and forgiveness."

> [If] My people who are called by My name humble themselves and pray and seek My face and turn from their wicked ways, then I will hear from heaven, will forgive their sin and will heal their land.
>
> 2 Chronicles 7:14 NASB
>
> A person's insight gives him patience, and his virtue is to overlook an offense.
>
> Proverbs 19:11 HCSB

Two years later, Lincoln wrote of a different kind of forgiveness—that which each person needed to extend to those who were their enemies during the Civil War.

"With Malice Toward None"

In his second inaugural speech, Lincoln said: "With malice toward none; with charity for all; with firmness in the right, as God gives us to see the right, let us strive on to finish the work we are in; to bind up the nation's wounds; to care for him who shall have borne the battle, and for his widow, and his orphan—to do all which may achieve and cherish a just, and a lasting peace, among ourselves, and with all nations."

Prayer and forgiveness—that's what set Lincoln's presidency apart, at a time when the country needed a great deal of both.

Further Insights

Lincoln's forgiveness was legendary. In 1857, Lincoln was to assist lawyer Edwin Stanton in defending a client, but Stanton snubbed Lincoln, calling him a "long-armed creature." After Lincoln became president, Stanton remarked that Washington was in disarray due to the "painful imbecility of Lincoln." Within the year, Lincoln appointed him secretary of war, believing him to be the best person for the job. He never mentioned Stanton's poor treatment of him.

Points to Remember

- Despite his position of power, Lincoln often realized that he had nowhere to turn but to God in prayer.

- Lincoln took the difficult route over the popular route in rebuking the country for its arrogance in forgetting God.

Sir Walter Raleigh's Last Prayer—Praying for Heaven

By all accounts, the legendary, dashing Walter Raleigh was quite the scoundrel. A pirate by profession in his younger years, Raleigh later garnered the good graces of Queen Elizabeth I, who knighted him in 1585 and gave him the prestigious position of captain of the guard. Sir Walter Raleigh was suddenly born, and he would make waves throughout the British Empire for the next three decades. Little did anyone think that this worldly courtier and adventurer would utter a profound prayer to repentance as he anticipated the blow of the executioner's ax.

Raleigh's Achievements

Raleigh's achievements are nearly as impressive as the number of his sins. He may have introduced potatoes to Ireland, explored Virginia, and fought against the Spanish Armada.

An accomplished poet, he may have written poems attributed to Shakespeare; literary scholar C. S. Lewis reserved high praise for Raleigh's unembellished style. While imprisoned, Raleigh began writing a multivolume history of the world.

> How long, O men, will you turn my glory into shame? How long will you love delusions and seek false gods? Know that the LORD has set apart the godly for himself; the LORD will hear when I call to him. In your anger do not sin; when you are on your beds, search your hearts and be silent.
>
> Psalm 4:2–4 NIV

Then, too, he quelled colonial rebellion by having dissidents killed, and he operated a brothel where mocking God provided a secondary means of entertainment. He fathered a child with one of the queen's maids, costing him royal favor. Following Elizabeth's death, King James sentenced him to death for treason and insubordination.

"Forgive Me"

At his execution in October 1618, Raleigh addressed the assembled crowd, denying the charges and affirming his allegiance to the Crown. Finally, he spoke to God: "Now I entreat you all to join with me in prayer, that the great God of Heaven, whom I have grievously offended, being a man full of all vanity, and having lived a sinful life, in all sinful callings, having been a soldier, a captain, a sea captain, and a courtier, which are all places of wickedness and vice; that God, I say, would forgive me, cast away my sins from me, and receive me into everlasting life. So I take my leave of you all, making my peace with God."

With that, Raleigh became as the thief on the cross—a sinner who finally recognized the sovereignty of God when it mattered most.

Digging Deeper

The two condemned criminals at Jesus' crucifixion had radically different responses to Christ. One mocked him: "Some Messiah you are! Save yourself! Save us!" The other, however, feared God: "Have you no fear of God? You're getting the same as him," he said. "We deserve this, but not him—he did nothing to deserve this." And then he turned to Jesus, saying, "Jesus, remember me when you enter your kingdom" (Luke 23:39-42 MSG). Jesus assured him that he would. Foxhole conversions, deathbed conversions, guillotine conversions—only God can judge them, but Jesus gave them credibility.

Further Insights

Several accounts of Sir Walter Raleigh's execution indicate that after Raleigh rested his head on the chopping block, someone standing nearby noticed that his head was facing west and suggested that he turn his head toward the east—the Holy Land. Raleigh replied, "What matter how the head lie, if the heart be right?"

A Civil War Soldier's Prayer—
Praying for the Wrong Things

Some skeptics believe that if there is a God he probably sits around on a cloud removed from the lives and problems of the humans he created. Not so. God has your best interests in mind and is involved in your life even from before birth. You might feel alone and unable to reach him, but he hears your prayers and answers them with firmness and compassion. A soldier serving in the Confederate Army during the American Civil War caught a glimpse of God's intentions before dying on the field of battle.

✵

July 1863—Gettysburg, Pennsylvania

General Robert E. Lee shifted in his saddle and surveyed his soldiers and the opposition amassed near the small college town. The Union Army of the Potomac had a new commander, General George Meade. Meade brought a cadre of 94,000 men along with their new Spencer repeating carbine rifles to bear against Lee's 72,000. The Union's lines ran south-to-north along Cemetery Ridge and turned east to form a fishhook. On July 1, Lee's soldiers attacked the left flank, pushing the lines back into the town or the hills.

On the second day of the campaign, fierce fighting broke out on high ground. Union troops held firm to Little Round Top, Peach Orchard, and Wheat Field. At Devil's Den, a Confederate sharpshooter tucked himself into the rocks and harassed the charging Union troops, which gave the Confederates an opening to rally. To counter this pesky sharp-

> If any of you lacks wisdom, he should ask God, who gives to all generously and without criticizing, and it will be given to him.
>
> James 1:5 HCSB
>
> Everyone who asks, receives. Everyone who seeks, finds. And to everyone who knocks, the door will be opened.
>
> Matthew 7:8 NLT

shooter, Captain Augustus Martin of the Union V Corps artillery ordered a percussion shell strike. The blast killed the sharpshooter.

Thousands Dead

On July 3, Lee spearheaded 15,000 men into the Union lines at Cemetery Ridge. General George Pickett led 4,300 men in the now-famous  Pickett's Charge as part of this offensive. But Union artillery tangled their lines, which allowed them to flank the Confederates on three sides. The retreat left thousands of men dead, wounded, or stranded as prisoners. More than 7,800 men died in three days.

The Union had broken Lee's drive into the North. The war had turned.

How many men—in Blue and Gray—had prayed for victory, for safety, for peace, or for an end to the war? How can God respond amid the wounded flesh and scorched earth of war?

Insight into Prayer

A sliver of an answer was found on the battlefield. During the following days, the pungent odor of sulfur and gunpowder dissipated as the armies tended to their wounded and dead. Ammunition was collected. Foodstuffs and valuables were claimed as spoils. And a folded sheet of paper was found on a Confederate soldier who died near the fabled Devil's Den. History books will never list his name, but his insight into prayer—and the God who hears and answers—endures like one of the monuments erected to commemorate the battles.

"I asked God for strength, that I might achieve; I was made weak, that I might learn humbly to obey. I asked for health, that I might do great things; I was given infirmity, that I might do better things. I asked for riches, that I might be happy; I was given poverty, that I might be wise. I asked for power, that I might have the praise of men; I was given weakness, that I might feel the need of God. I asked for all things, that

I might enjoy life; I was given life, that I might enjoy all things. I got nothing that I asked for, but everything I had hoped for. Almost despite myself, my unspoken prayers were answered. I am, among all men, most richly blessed."

The soldier's observations were not forged in an afternoon; they were forged over months of seeking God in prayer.

Intent of Prayer

God is more concerned about the intent of your prayers than the content of your prayers. The soldier called out to God when he could have complained or cursed. God saw the soldier's heart and lavished his gifts on him.

> LORD, You have heard the desire of the humble; You will prepare their heart; You will cause Your ear to hear.
>
> Psalm 10:17 NKJV

God is openhanded out of love. God did not wait for the soldier to realize the wrong intent of his prayers. God responded out of his character. He is the one who does "immeasurably more than all we ask or imagine, according to his power that is at work within us" (Ephesians 3:20 NIV).

Civil War coins, belt buckles, uniforms, and weapons have all but disappeared, but the words of this soldier have endured. They stand like a battlefield monument to remind all who read them of the character and heart of God. God is listening to your prayers and answering according to his plan for your life. He is working to bless you.

Something to Ponder

Even Jesus prayed for the "wrong" things. The end of Jesus' earthly ministry was coming. After the Passover Feast, Jesus led his disciples to the garden of Gethsemane and asked them to keep watch while he prayed,

"O my Father, if it is possible, let this cup pass from Me; nevertheless, not as I will, but as You will" (Matthew 26:39 NKJV). The cup did not pass. Jesus was arrested, tried, wrongfully convicted, and executed according to Roman law. God was working out his ultimate plan to accomplish your salvation. In the same way, pray for what you desire, but do so with an attitude of, "nevertheless, not as I will, but as You will." God will take care of the rest.

Take It to Heart

Look at the lessons the Confederate soldier learned. For which of his requests have you prayed—strength, health, riches, power? Have you felt that God wasn't listening or responding? Take a few minutes to pray for the qualities the soldier received—humility, wisdom, joy. Allow his learned lessons to remodel your prayers.

Further Insights

Devil's Den got its name before the American Civil War. This collection of granite-like rocks has peaks that resemble a bat's ears. Emanuel Bushman, a local resident, recorded stories of a monstrous snake that lived in the cracks and crevices. They named the snake the Devil because it eluded those brave enough to hunt for it.  The outcropping soon became known as Devil's Den and is now immortalized in Civil War history.

The Book of Common Prayer—
Finding Words When You Have None

The Book of Common Prayer came out of the English Reformation. It is a compendium of written prayers, liturgies for various types of worship services, daily Bible readings, the book of Psalms, and other resources for public and private worship. It was born in 1549, revised in 1552 and 1559 and then again in 1662. Since that time it has had several major revisions, and the latest revision, the 1979 revision, is used today in the U.S. *The Book of Common Prayer* has been translated into nearly forty languages, including several Native American languages.

✳

For nearly four centuries, *The Book of Common Prayer* has been used for both public and private devotion. Its stately prayers blend Protestant interpretation with Catholic form, with many of its words and phrases becoming part of the language.

The Book of Common Prayer is a treasury of majestic prayers for:

- The world (for example, for peace, enemies, and "All Sorts and Conditions of Men")

- The church (for the clergy, the parish, and beyond)

- The nation (the government, elections, the military)

- The social order (cities, rural areas, the unemployed)

- The natural order (creation, conservation, the harvest)

- Family and personal life (children, the elderly, travelers, victims of addiction)

> Each day the LORD pours his unfailing love upon me, and through each night I sing his songs, praying to God who gives me life.
>
> Psalm 42:8 NLT
>
> Very early in the morning, while it was still dark, He got up, went out, and made His way to a deserted place. And He was praying there.
>
> Mark 1:35 HCSB

- Other prayers (preparation for mealtimes, worship services, Communion)

Although it is considered a literary masterpiece, *The Book of Common Prayer* doesn't ignore the ordinary routines of everyday life. Its readers know that after a stressful day, they can take a deep breath, turn to "Other Prayers," and find these words: "O Lord, support us all the day long, until the shadows lengthen, and the evening comes, and the busy world is hushed, and the fever of life is over, and our work is done. Then in your mercy, grant us a safe lodging, and a holy rest, and peace at the last."

In all, the personal prayer section offers seventy prayers for various situations, celebrations, demographics, and difficulties—in essence, a prayer for nearly every purpose.

Myth Buster

Some Christians believe written prayers are lifeless, while others consider them to be unbiblical because Jesus didn't use written prayers. The reality is that the Psalms are the written prayers of the Bible and have served as a life-giving prayer book for Jews and Christians for centuries. And every day, all around the world, Christians pray a universal, written prayer, the Lord's Prayer, written in the gospels of Matthew and Luke.

Digging Deeper

The Book of Common Prayer includes the Daily Offices—special prayers for morning, noon, evening, and close of day. There's also a special section of Daily Offices for families with young children and short attention spans. And there's a lot of flexibility and variations, some of which require using *The Book of Common Prayer* and the Bible.

Profiles in Prayer

To these great teachers on the subject of prayer, all their combined words about prayer were of little consequence when compared to even a few words spoken in prayer to God.

Contents

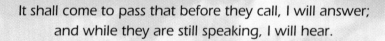

It shall come to pass that before they call, I will answer;
and while they are still speaking, I will hear.

Isaiah 65:24 NKJV

E. M. Bounds—How to Endure in Prayer

To the larger world in the nineteenth century, E. M. (Edward McKendree) Bounds was at various times an attorney, a Methodist pastor, a chaplain with a regiment of the Confederate States Army, a prisoner of an itinerant pastor, an editor of several Christian magazines, an author, and an evangelist. Regardless of what may have been written on his résumé, E. M. Bounds had one job throughout his adulthood: he prayed. No matter where he was, no matter who was with him, no matter who might be disturbed, he rose at 4 a.m. and prayed for at least three hours.

✻

According to those who knew him best, few people could match Bounds's intensity and disciplined nature. "He prayed, for long years, upon subjects which the easy-going Christian rarely gives a thought, and for objects which men of less thought and faith are always ready to call impossible," Claude Chilton Jr. wrote in the foreword to one of Bounds's seven books on prayer, *The Necessity of Prayer*.

> We will devote ourselves to prayer and to the preaching ministry.
>
> Acts 6:4 HCSB
>
> Never give up. Eagerly follow the Holy Spirit and serve the Lord. Let your hope make you glad. Be patient in time of trouble and never stop praying.
>
> Romans 12:11–12 CEV

Prayer as a Reflex Action

Chilton, a longtime admirer of Bounds, wrote that to Bounds, prayer was a reflex action; it came as naturally to him as breathing comes to ordinary humans. Others may say they believe people can do nothing without prayer, he added, but Bounds took that principle literally and lived it out every day of his life. "Faith, and hope, and patience and all the strong, beautiful, vital forces of piety are withered and dead in a prayerless life," Bounds once wrote. Not praying was simply not an option.

And yet he was well aware that the majority of Christians in his church, in his community, in his revival meetings, were not people of prayer, either out of ignorance or laziness. He had every intention of curing them of both afflictions, the first by teaching on prayer at every available opportunity, and the second by preaching the idleness out of them. He had little problem holding others to the high standards he held for himself; when a soul was at stake, nothing else mattered.

Prayer as a Life's Work

To say that prayer was his life's work is no exaggeration. It was his job, his career. "Prayer is a trade to be learned," Bounds wrote. "We must be apprentices and serve our time at it. Painstaking care, much thought, practice, and labor are required to be a skillful tradesman in praying. Practice in this, as well as in all other trades, makes perfect." Bounds was a pietist, and as such perfectionism characterized his quest to be holy.

The goal of prayer, he maintained, was to reach the ear of God, and that was worth all the time and effort a person could put into it. Enduring in prayer meant "patient and continued and continuous waiting upon Him," something he saw little of in the people around him: "I think Christians fail so often to get answers to their prayers because they do not wait long enough on God. They just drop down and say a few words, and then jump up and forget it and expect God to answer them. Such praying always reminds me of the small boy ringing his neighbor's doorbell, and then running away as fast as he can go."

Prayerless Preachers

Power Through Prayer, a book by Bounds that was finished posthumously, was directed at prayerless preachers, another group Bounds thought was much too large. His pietist leanings left him with little patience for preachers who spent more time studying the writings of biblical scholars than they did actually reading the Bible or praying. No matter how successful a ministry might be, if it was not undergirded by hours of daily prayer, its efforts were useless.

Upon his death in 1913, only two of his books had been published, and while he was well-known in his immediate circles, he was best-known as the former associate editor of a newspaper, the *Nashville Christian Advocate*. Claude Chilton took up the task of completing the remaining books on prayer that Bounds had been unable to finish, and they brought E. M. Bounds recognition as an authority on prayer for decades after he died. Chilton wrote this of his books: "These books are unfailing wells for a lifetime of spiritual water-drawing. They are hidden treasures, wrought in the darkness of dawn and the heat of the noon, on the anvil of experience, and beaten into wondrous form by the mighty stroke of the divine. They are living voices whereby he, being dead, yet speaketh!"

> We desire that each one of you show the same diligence so as to realize the full assurance of hope until the end, so that you will not be sluggish, but imitators of those who through faith and patience inherit the promises.
>
> Hebrews 6:11–12 NASB

Digging Deeper

A Methodist, E. M. Bounds adhered to a form of spirituality known as pietism, which had its roots in Germany and emphasized inner experience, personal faith, a literal interpretation of Scripture, and a return to practices mentioned in the New Testament such as foot-washing and greeting one another with a holy  kiss. Pietists believed in relying on the Spirit's revelation rather than commentaries in their study of Scripture; and their faith was rooted more in practice—leading a holy life of religious commitment—rather than doctrine. Well-known pietists include Puritan preacher Jonathan Edwards and John Wesley, the founder of Methodism.

Further Insights

Twice in his life, E. M. Bounds was incarcerated. Bounds was a pastor in Missouri when the Civil War reached the state. Union forces imprisoned Bounds as a suspected Confederate sympathizer and transferred him to Alabama. After his release, he walked a hundred miles to a Confederate camp and was sworn in as a chaplain. After a losing battle in Franklin, Tennessee, Bounds refused to leave the casualties on the battlefield, aware that Union troops would again arrest him. Six months later, Bounds was released and returned to Franklin, where he started a church that flourished and grew after the war ended.

Check Your Understanding

- **What did Bounds consider his life's work to be?**

Bounds looked upon prayer as a job that required diligence, patience, and endurance. Every person who was disciplined in praying was an apprentice whose task was to practice his trade and continually get better at it.

- **For what group in particular did E. M. Bounds reserve some of his hardest words?**

Pastors came under particular scrutiny. He knew many pastors who placed little priority on prayer, and he believed that their ministries would ultimately prove to be fruitless.

- **What did Bounds think was the main reason the prayers of Christians weren't answered?**

He felt that most Christians failed to spend enough time in prayer at any given time. Instead of waiting patiently on the Lord, they prayed a quick prayer, turned to other things, and expected results.

Oswald Chambers—
How to Get to Know God Through Prayer

Daily devotionals have long held a special place in the hearts and lives of Christians. Throughout their history, the content of a typical devotional has expanded from formal opportunities for deep teaching to more light-hearted and casual observations about everyday contemporary life.

Some devotionals barely outlast the season in which they were published. But one has remained in print, and in constant use, since 1927: *My Utmost for His Highest* by Scottish preacher Oswald Chambers.

✳

The words of *My Utmost* are those of Chambers, but it is to his wife that readers owe a debt of gratitude. An accomplished stenographer, Biddy Chambers recorded her husband's talks and began compiling them in devotional form following his death in 1917.

In the foreword to the book, she wrote, "This book has been . . . sent out with the prayer that day by day the messages may continue to bring the quickening life and inspiration of the Holy Spirit." Her prayer was clearly answered, given the book's long publishing history.

Answered Prayer

Answered prayer was never a surprise to Oswald Chambers. His expectation of answered prayer

Everyone who partakes only of milk is not accustomed to the word of righteousness, for he is an infant. But solid food is for the mature, who because of practice have their senses trained to discern good and evil.

Hebrews 5:13–14 NASB

When I am among mature believers, I do speak with words of wisdom, but not the kind of wisdom that belongs to this world or to the rulers of this world, who are soon forgotten.

1 Corinthians 2:6 NLT

was unwavering. And though he held himself and other Christians to an exceedingly high standard, he was not above using subtle, wry humor to get his message across. Here's this, from the April 16 entry in *My Utmost for His Highest*: "Never allow a feeling which was stirred in you in the high hour to evaporate. Don't put your mental feet on the mantelpiece and say—'What a marvellous state of mind to be in!' Act immediately . . . don't say—'I'll do it'; *do it*! Take yourself by the scruff of the neck and shake off your incarnate laziness."

Deeper Teachings of the Gospel

Hebrews 5 and 1 Corinthians 3 speak to those who are not ready for solid food—the deeper teachings of the gospel. If you've had your fill of milk—devotionals that appeal to people new to the faith—it may be time for some solid devotional food, the kind Oswald Chambers dished out.

Something to Ponder

One of Oswald Chambers's primary concerns was the lack of concern for holiness among professing Christians. Today, the word *holiness* has an antiquated, stuffy ring to it, something that would horrify Chambers. "Holiness, not happiness, is the chief end of man," he maintained. But maybe it's the word and not the concept that poses a problem for twenty-first-century Christians. How can you incorporate a contemporary understanding of holiness into your life?

Final Thoughts

If your busy life has interfered with your reading life, consider reading a daily devotional. The chapters are short, and the Internet makes it easy to keep up with the daily entries. Older devotionals like *My Utmost for His Highest* are available free online, and entries can be delivered daily to your in-box where they will be waiting for you if you oversleep or forget to read them before you leave the house.

George Mueller—
Praying When the Odds Are Against You

Nineteenth-century England saw the rise of intellectualism in the church. Religious scholars scrutinized each facet of faith to determine if it made sense; what didn't make sense was discarded or relegated to "meaningless but innocuous" status. They looked at prayer from a logical, rational perspective and debated whether the practice had any merit at all. Some concluded that its value lay only in the comfort it brought to those who prayed. Meanwhile, in the city of Bristol, an unassuming pastor with an astonishing faith in God was shaking the religious landscape by ignoring the debate and simply praying.

✳

Life of Trust in God

Stories about the life of George Mueller would seem mythical if there wasn't such thorough documentation to back them up. Newspaper accounts, contemporaneous journals, letters, ledgers, and other writings attest to Mueller's astounding life of trust in God. Through prayer alone, Mueller accomplished what all the rest of England seemed incapable of doing: taking care of the country's many orphans.

Judging from his early life, Mueller wasn't a likely candidate for any kind of altruistic endeavor. By the age of fourteen, he had acquired a taste for alcohol and gambling. That was his age when his mother died;

This is the confidence that we have in Him, that if we ask anything according to His will, He hears us. And if we know that He hears us, whatever we ask, we know that we have the petitions that we have asked of Him.

1 John 5:14–15 NKJV

Seek His kingdom, and these things will be provided for you. Don't be afraid, little flock, because your Father delights to give you the kingdom.

Luke 12:31–32 HCSB

young George continued drinking and gambling with his friends as she lay on her deathbed.

Evangelical Friends

And he was a chronic liar and an incorrigible thief—until he enrolled in divinity school, which he did to deceive his father into thinking he had changed his evil ways. But it wasn't his theological studies that caused him to give up his life of debauchery; it was the influence of a group of evangelical friends that led him to a relationship with Jesus.

During the early years of his pastorate in Bristol, he came to better understand the ministry of the Holy Spirit, particularly with regard to

relying on the Spirit for scriptural revelation. "The result of this was, that the first evening that I shut myself into my room to give myself to prayer and meditation over the Scriptures, I learned more in a few hours than I had done during a period of several months previously," he wrote.

Immediately Mueller made some radical changes. He declined taking a salary from the church. He determined that he would never let anyone but God and his wife know about any need he or his ministry had, and sometimes he even left his wife out of the conversation. He resolved never to take out a loan or amass any other kind of debt.

And yet, with fifty cents in seed money, George Mueller built orphanages that housed as many as two thousand children at a time; over the course of sixty years, he fed, clothed, educated, and trained the children for employment, without asking for a penny from anyone. He simply prayed.

Unsolicited Provision

On several occasions, there was little or no food in the pantry, certainly not enough to feed two thousand children. But always, some unsolicited provision would arrive at the last minute; on one occasion, the children had assembled in the dining hall and had just found their places at the table when the food that was needed for their meal miraculously arrived at the kitchen door. *"How* the means are to come, I know not; but I know that God is almighty, that the hearts of all are in His hands, and that, if He pleaseth to influence persons, they will send help," Mueller once wrote. The children never went hungry.

> Dispense true justice and practice kindness and compassion each to his brother; and do not oppress the widow or the orphan, the stranger or the poor; and do not devise evil in your hearts against one another.
>
> Zechariah 7:9–10 NASB

Despite all the evidence that Mueller was a man of remarkable faith, he insisted that he did not have the "gift of faith" mentioned in 1 Corinthians 12:9. His reason? He never wanted other Christians to think he had some special gift. He wanted his faith in God to encourage and inspire others to trust God to the same extent—and to pray with the same confidence with which he prayed.

Mueller's prayers for God's tangible provision were widely known, but his journals also mention the daily problems that plagued the orphanages. He depended on God for every troubling matter that arose. In everything, he prayed for one purpose: that God would be glorified.

"Patient, persevering, believing prayer, offered up to God, in the Name of the Lord Jesus, has always, sooner or later, brought the blessing," he wrote. "I do not despair, by God's grace, of obtaining any blessing, provided I can be sure it would be for any real good, and for the glory of God."

Further Insights

George Mueller's accomplishments are daunting to twenty-first-century believers, and yet he lived in the nineteenth century. Among his achievements:

- He started more than 100 schools and educated 120,000 children.

- Between the ages of seventy and eighty-seven, he traveled two hundred thousand miles—long before the age of airplane travel.

- He addressed three million people in his lifetime.

- He was pastor of the same church for sixty-six years.

- For nearly fifty years, he read through the Bible four times each year.

- He became so well known and so beloved that tens of thousands of people attended his funeral.

Points to Remember

- Instead of getting involved in the religious debate of the day, George Mueller quietly proved the power of prayer through his day-to-day routine.

- Mueller simply believed God, devoted much of his time to prayer and Bible reading, and wanted only to glorify God.

- He did not have any special kind of gift; the faith he had is available to everyone.

Something to Ponder

Imagine what would happen today if someone like George Mueller moved into your neighborhood, started attending your church, and went before the appropriate authorities to get building permits, licensing, and other permissions to build an orphanage—by faith alone. How do you think each of those groups—the community, the church, the governmental bodies—would perceive such a person?

Stormie Omartian—
The Power of Praying for Others

At a time of intense struggle in her marriage, singer Stormie Omartian prayed what she called her favorite three-word prayer: "Change him, Lord." When God failed to change her husband, Omartian humbled herself and uttered a different three-word prayer that changed everything: "Lord, change me." Little did Omartian know that seeking transformation for herself would propel her into a worldwide ministry of intercessory prayer. In the past decade, millions of Christians have turned to her books and her ministry to discover the power of praying for others.

✳

To look at her today, you wouldn't suspect that this attractive, polished woman experienced a hard life. Growing up on a remote Wyoming ranch, the young Stormie was so ashamed of her family's poverty and her mother's abusive behavior that she distanced herself from any potential friends.

If you sinful people know how to give good gifts to your children, how much more will your heavenly Father give the Holy Spirit to those who ask him.

Luke 11:13 NLT

Thank GOD for his marvelous love, for his miracle mercy to the children he loves.

Psalm 107:8 MSG

Synonymous with Intercessory Prayer

As an adult, Stormie turned to God and began to truly heal from the memories of the emotional abuse and the physical abuse that her mother had inflicted on her. When she did, all heaven broke loose. And when she began writing on prayer, Omartian found her calling. *The Power of a Praying Parent* started things off in 1995. But *The Power of a Praying Wife*, published two years later, resonated with so many readers that her name became synonymous with intercessory prayer. In the book, she offered a candid glimpse into the problems in her own marriage to well-known singer and songwriter Michael Omartian.

Authenticity

Her authenticity drew readers to subsequent books that followed the "power of a praying . . ." format, directed at husbands, women, children, the nation, the church, and other demographics. Her readers often say they close her books with a newfound commitment to praying for other people.

If that's the case, then Omartian has fulfilled her purpose in writing her many books on prayer: "Far too often prayer becomes a complicated issue for people. . . . In all the books I have written, I have sought to dispel that kind of fear and intimidation and make prayer accessible to everyone."

Something to Ponder

In *The Prayer That Changes Everything*, Omartian wrote this: "Worship and praise is the *purest* form of prayer because it focuses our minds and souls entirely away from ourselves and on to Him." Think about the times you have immersed yourself in prayer of this type. Were you able to take the focus entirely off yourself, and if so, for how long?

Further Insights

Omartian emphasized the need to prayerfully seek to understand the people you are praying for—especially when praying for a spouse. God understands your spouse better than your spouse does, so asking God to give you wisdom and understanding enables you to pray accord-  ing to God's will for your husband or wife. And no matter whom you are praying for, a deeper understanding of a person's struggles gives you greater compassion for him or her.

Andrew Murray—Prayer Is More Than Maintaining the Status Quo

In nineteenth-century South Africa, a young pastor began to put down on paper his thoughts about the Christian life. By the time he died in 1917 at the age of eighty-eight, he had written 240 books, plus numerous essays and articles. His name was Andrew Murray, and to this day believers continue to cherish his books. Among the best known is *With Christ in the School of Prayer*, a call to a deeper prayer life organized into thirty-one lessons taken from New Testament teachings on prayer.

✳

Murray was concerned over the health of Christians' prayer lives and their ignorance about the power and purpose of prayer. Too many people he knew prayed only because that was what Christians were expected to do. "I feel sure that as long as we look on prayer chiefly as the means of maintaining our own Christian life, we shall not know fully what it is meant to be," he wrote.

Evening and morning and at noon I will pray, and cry aloud, and He shall hear my voice.

Psalm 55:17 NKJV

I pray that Christ Jesus and the church will forever bring praise to God. His power at work in us can do far more than we dare ask or imagine. Amen.

Ephesians 3:20–21 CEV

Prayer as the Highest Work

Discovering "what it is meant to be" became Murray's life work—in addition to preaching, pastoring, doing social work (he served as the first president of the YMCA, at that time known for its commitment to changing society), founding educational institutions, and, of course, writing. First and foremost, Murray regarded prayer as the "highest work" entrusted to Jesus' followers.

Chief among his many concerns about Christians was their lack of an unwavering faith, and hence their lack of a believing prayer life. "We have become so accustomed to limit the wonderful love and the large promises of our God," he wrote, "that we cannot read the simplest and clearest statements of our Lord without the qualifying clauses by which we guard and expound them." There was never any doubt in anyone's mind that Andrew Murray refused to limit God's love or qualify his promises.

Powerful Things Can Be accomplished

Murray thoroughly believed that through prayer many powerful things could be accomplished:

- Believers can occupy a place of power and influence.

- A weary world can be transformed.

- God will fulfill his promise to grant whatever is asked in Jesus' name.

- Both the "feeblest child" and the holiest saint can communicate with God on the same terms.

- Christians can have fellowship with the Most High God.

- Believers can grab hold of God and draw on his strength.

- The promises that are waiting to be fulfilled will finally find their fulfillment.

- The art of effectual prayer can be learned under the guidance of the Holy Spirit.

That's just a start. Murray genuinely believed that anything could be accomplished through prayer, and he lived his life accordingly. Those who heard him preach often compared him to the thundering prophets of the Old Testament, despite his frail appearance. And those who happened to meet him on the street couldn't help but think that he was searching for some evidence of God's work in their lives.

But that hadn't always been the case. For the first ten years of his life as a Christian, some of those years spent as a pastor, he was restless and discontent: "My thoughts, my words, my actions, my faithfulness—everything troubled me. Though all around thought me one of the most earnest of men, my life was one of deep dissatisfaction. I struggled and prayed as best I could."

> Be gracious to me, Lord, for I call to You all day long.
>
> Psalm 86:3 HCSB

Daily Act of Surrender

Over time, Murray learned an important lesson, one that changed his life and transformed his ministry: he learned to place himself at God's disposal every morning, "as a vessel to be filled with His Holy Spirit." That daily act of surrender, and remaining in submission throughout the day, proved to Murray that it was indeed God who was now doing the work that Murray had been trying to do on his own.

And yet, Murray remained restless. He had become restless at the thought of all that awaited him in the presence of God. The closer he drew to God in prayer, the more he realized that a much fuller revelation of God's grace lay just beyond his earthly grasp. "Let us never hesitate to say, This is only the beginning. When we are brought into the holiest of all, we are only beginning to take our right position with the Father."

Ever since Murray wrote his first book in the late 1800s, Christians have cherished the words he wrote. His are the kind of books that end up underlined, dog-eared, and falling apart. Following are some of his best-known words about prayer.

The Words of Andrew Murray

Topic	Quotation
Expectation	Think of what He can do, and how He delights to hear the prayers of His redeemed people. Think of your place and privilege in Christ, and expect great things!
Faith	Faith in a prayer-hearing God will make a prayer-loving Christian.
God's presence	Let this be your chief object in prayer, to realize the presence of your heavenly Father.
Knowing God	Some people pray just to pray and some people pray to know God.
Listening	Prayer is not monologue, but dialogue. God's voice in response to mine is its most essential part.
Mystery of prayer	We must begin to believe that God, in the mystery of prayer, has entrusted us with a force that can move the Heavenly world, and can bring its power down to earth.
Reward	Let it be your business every day, in the secrecy of the inner chamber, to meet the holy God. You will be repaid for the trouble it may cost you. The reward will be sure and rich.
Submission	When we pray for the Spirit's help . . . we will simply fall down at the Lord's feet in our weakness. There we will find the victory and power that comes from His love.
Thankfulness	Thanksgiving will draw our hearts out to God and keep us engaged with Him; it will take our attention from ourselves and give the Spirit room in our hearts.
Unceasing prayer	If the spiritual life be healthy, under the full power of the Holy Spirit, praying without ceasing will be natural.
Unexpected	Beware in your prayers, above everything else, of limiting God, not only by unbelief, but by fancying that you know what He can do. Expect unexpected things "above all that we ask or think."
Work	Time spent in prayer will yield more than that given to work. Prayer alone gives work its worth and its success. Prayer opens the way for God Himself to do His work in us and through us.

Evelyn Christenson—
What Happens When You Pray?

For Evelyn Christenson—author of the best-selling book *What Happens When Women Pray?*—prayer is inseparable from both the Bible and evangelism. She believes the Bible inspires people to pray and gives them the wisdom to know how to pray, and she believes praying for the lost needs to be a priority for all Christians. Inseparable from prayer is love. Christenson's prayers are bathed in love for God, for other Christians, and for those who don't yet know God.

✳

A Prayer Growing Deep

One of Christenson's Bible-reading methods may seem peculiar to those who follow a structured Scripture-reading plan: she reads only until she senses God speaking to her, and then she meditates on that passage until she can apply its wisdom to her life. Sometimes she will dwell on one verse for days. But all the while, a prayer is growing deep within her, and often that application and that prayer lead her to a deeper love for nonbelievers.

Given that, you would think she would favor any evangelistic method. Not so. Christenson believes that evangelism needs to be preceded by a specific way of praying, asking God to get involved and removing the blinders from the eyes of those who have been unable to see God's truth. That prayer needs to be accompanied by genuine love, compassion, and kindness toward the unbelieving person.

> I am giving you a new commandment: Love each other. Just as I have loved you, you should love each other.
>
> John 13:34 NLT

> Let us love one another, because love is from God, and everyone who loves has been born of God and knows God.
>
> 1 John 4:7 HCSB

A Pattern for Praying

After thirty-plus years of organizing prayer retreats, meetings, conferences, and small groups, Christenson developed a pattern for praying with and for others that she believes will revolutionize the lives of those praying and those prayed for:

- Find two prayer partners and pray with them weekly.

- Ask each partner to pray for three other people to come to Christ.

- Perform acts of kindness toward those being prayed for.

- Keep praying for and loving those nine people until they come to Christ.

Christenson reminds those who are praying evangelistically to pray for one another—a vital factor in any evangelistic effort.

Anyone involved in an evangelistic prayer ministry, one that places highest priority on bringing people into a personal relationship with Jesus Christ, has likely heard that question. Sometimes outsiders ask the question derisively, but many seek a deeper understanding of the need to pray for nonbelievers. The following chart shows what the Bible has to say.

Why Pray Evangelistically?

Scripture	Reason to Pray
Matthew 24:14	Jesus will return—but only after the good news about the kingdom of God reaches the entire world.
Matthew 28:18–20 Mark 16:15	Jesus commanded his followers to go out into the world and make disciples of all nations.
Luke 24:46–47 Acts 1:8	Jesus told his followers to be witnesses for him in every part of the world, no matter how remote.
1 Timothy 2:4 Titus 2:11 2 Peter 3:9	God wants everyone to come to a saving knowledge of the truth.
1 John 2:2 Revelation 7:9–10	Jesus' atonement was for the whole world, but the whole world doesn't know it.
Revelation 5:8–9	People from every nation around the world will be present at the scene of Jesus' final victory in heaven.

Richard Foster—Communion with God

For some people, only one image comes to mind when they hear the word *Quaker*. They think of a kind-looking man wearing austere clothing—an image straight from an oatmeal box. But those familiar with the Society of Friends know that while kindness is a hallmark of Quakerism, austerity is not. As a Quaker, Richard Foster grew up in an environment that encouraged freedom rather than rigidity in his prayer life. Today, millions of readers have benefited from his freedom to explore prayer in all its dimensions. Many credit him with renewing their dormant prayer lives.

In writing about prayer, Foster admitted to being a novice. "Who can ever master something in which the main purpose is to be mastered?" he asked in the preface to one of his best-known books, *Prayer: Finding the Heart's True Home*. But this "novice" has served as an experienced guide to countless Christians who want to explore the nature of prayer and the way different types of prayer can help them overcome the obstacles they face in actually praying. His is hardly a lofty, high-minded approach: "Healthy prayer necessitates frequent experiences of the common, earthy, run-of-the-mill variety—experiences like walks, talks, and good wholesome laughter; like work in the yard, chitchat with neighbors, and washing windows; like loving your spouse, playing with the kids, and working with your colleagues."

> Sing to Him, sing psalms to Him; talk of all His wondrous works!
>
> 1 Chronicles 16:9 NKJV
>
> One thing I have asked from the LORD, that I shall seek: that I may dwell in the house of the LORD all the days of my life, to behold the beauty of the LORD and to meditate in His temple.
>
> Psalm 27:4 NASB

Communion with God

Foster does not doubt that God answers prayer, but he believes the primary purpose of prayer is communion with God; prayers that seek and expect answers naturally grow from that intimate relationship. Being one with the Spirit and then knowing how to pray and what to pray for will become second nature.

After a lifetime of prayer and studying prayer, Foster organized prayer into the following categories, to serve as helpful explanations and descriptions rather than rigid formats.

Richard Foster's Twenty-one Types of Prayer

Type of Prayer	Description
Adoration	Worship
Authoritative	Calling forth the will of God upon the earth
Contemplative	Wordless saturation in the presence of God
Covenant	Unswerving allegiance and holy obedience to God
Examination	Examining your heart and your daily encounters with God
Formation	Being conformed to Christ's image by the power of the Spirit
Forsaken	Searching for a seemingly absent God
Healing	Seeking restoration of health for yourself or others
Heart	Intimacy with God
Intercessory	Making requests for others
Meditative	Deep focus on the truth of Scripture
Ordinary	Turning ordinary experiences into prayer
Petitions	Making requests for yourself
Radical	Believing that people, institutions, and societies can be transformed
Relinquishment	Not your will but God's will
Rest	Serenity amid chaos and unrest
Sacramental	Incarnational prayer that accompanies Communion
Simple	Come as you are, honest and vulnerable
Suffering	Immersing yourself in others' trials and giving God your own difficulties
Tears	Personal repentance and sorrow for the sins of the world
Unceasing	Practicing the presence of God throughout the day

C. S. Lewis—The Primary Objective of Prayer

In addition to being a noted Cambridge literary scholar, C. S. Lewis was among the best-known converts to Christianity in the twentieth century. By his own admission, he came to faith reluctantly and after a long and difficult struggle. The fruit of that struggle was a mind that grappled with spiritual reality and shared the resulting observations with readers far beyond the walls of academia. Whatever conclusions Lewis reached about prayer, he came about honestly. Lewis was never one to speak down to his audience, and when he wrote about prayer, his questions about the subject revealed his humility and vulnerability.

✳

As a child, Lewis rejected the notion of a loving, prayer-answering God after his mother died of cancer despite his own fervent prayers. He became a Christian two decades later, and two decades after that he attempted to write a book on prayer but soon abandoned the project. Still, he addressed the topic of prayer in most of his books, most notably in *The Screwtape Letters*, in which a senior devil teaches a junior devil how to trip up the Christian he is bedeviling.

Two People Helping Each Other

That book breathed new life into his manuscript on prayer, which eventually became *Letters to Malcolm: Chiefly About Prayer*, a slim volume of imagined correspondence between two people helping each other understand the purpose of prayer. In one letter to Malcolm,

> Once Jesus was in a certain place praying. As he finished, one of his disciples came to him and said, "Lord, teach us to pray, just as John taught his disciples."
>
> Luke 11:1 NLT
>
> With every prayer and request, pray at all times in the Spirit, and stay alert in this, with all perseverance and intercession for all the saints. Pray also for me, that the message may be given to me when I open my mouth to make known with boldness the mystery of the gospel.
>
> Ephesians 6:18–19 HCSB

Lewis wrote: "However badly needed a good book on prayer is, I shall never try to write it. Two people on the foothills comparing notes in private are all very well. But in a book one would inevitably seem to be attempting, not discussion, but instruction. And for me to offer the world instruction about prayer would be impudence." He had little tolerance for his own impudence; *Letters to Malcolm* reads much more like the private notes of two people on the foothills than a how-to on prayer.

Difficult Theological Concepts

Lewis's brilliance lay in part in the effortless way he distilled difficult theological concepts into readily understood images. In *Mere Christianity*, likely his most widely read book, he presented an image of prayer that also described the Trinity.

Imagine, he suggested, a Christian kneeling in prayer, trying to get in touch with God. He's reaching out in prayer, but he's also aware that the inclination to pray came from within—from the Holy Spirit prompting him to pray. And he's aware that Christ is present, helping him pray and interceding on his behalf. Lewis wrote: "The whole threefold life of the three-personal Being is actually going on in that ordinary little bedroom where an ordinary man is saying his prayers. The man is being caught up into the higher kinds of life . . . he is being pulled into God, by God, while still remaining himself."

A person prays to God, through the prompting of the Holy Spirit, with Jesus at his side. Lewis used one simple illustration to explain two complex subjects, prayer and the Trinity.

Prayer, Bible Study, and Fasting

Given Lewis's prolific literary output, which included more than thirty books and countless articles, essays, and radio scripts, his academic responsibilities, and his correspondence with scholars, students, readers, and fans, he could be forgiven had he let his own spiritual disciplines slip a bit. But by all accounts, he never did. Lewis devoted many hours to prayer, Bible study, and fasting each week.

Even so, Lewis recognized prayer for the sacrifice of time and self that it is, once remarking that only in heaven will people find true pleasure in prayer. To Lewis, prayer sometimes seemed like work—and his honesty in admitting that helped people to realize that they were not alone in their struggles with prayer. He also felt the constant tug of distractions and found that at times he could remain focused only by praying the written prayers in the Anglican *Book of Common Prayer*.

> I will give you my message in the form of a vision. Write it clearly enough to be read at a glance. At the time I have decided, my words will come true. You can trust what I say about the future. It may take a long time, but keep on waiting—it will happen!
>
> Habakkuk 2:2–3 CEV

Praying Through the Book of Psalms

One other prayer discipline Lewis is believed to have followed is the practice of praying through the book of Psalms each month, something that Christians, and Jews, have done for millennia. To pray all 150 psalms in thirty days requires praying five psalms a day—a daunting undertaking for an early twentieth-century British professor as well as for an early twenty-first-century American citizen.

Though the temptation to do so must have been great, Lewis resisted the urge to pray mindlessly when he prayed the psalms or written prayers. "Simply to say prayers is not to pray," he wrote. "Otherwise a team of properly trained parrots would serve as well."

Further Insights

Quotes from *Letters to Malcolm*:

• "Creation seems to be delegation through and through. He will do nothing of Himself which can be done by creatures. I suppose this is because He is a giver. And He has nothing to give but Himself."

- "I still think that prayer without words is the best—if one can really achieve it. But I now see that in trying to make it my daily bread I was counting on a greater mental and spiritual strength than I really have."

- "There is always hope if we keep an unsolved problem fairly in view; there's none if we pretend it's not there."

Something to Ponder

 Despite his many other responsibilities, C. S. Lewis made a commitment to personally answer every letter that required a response. When his popularity as a writer reached its peak, he received as many as three hundred letters a week. If the letter writer asked a question, Lewis felt obligated to answer, offering clarification on something he'd written or advice to aspiring writers, for example. If you suddenly became famous, could you follow through on such a commitment?

Final Thoughts

Some Christians find it difficult to admit to the struggles they have with prayer. They may be afraid to appear less spiritual than other Christians. Or they may be concerned that their questions could cause new Christians to doubt God. But being open and honest about any faith challenge can often help others feel as if they are not alone in their struggles and open the door for you to minister to them.

Catherine Marshall—Don't Just Believe in Prayer, Pray

To the public at large, Catherine Marshall was the author of two best-selling books that became screen adaptations: *A Man Called Peter,* which was made into a movie in 1955; and *Christy,* a TV series that aired from 1994 to 1995. But among Christian readers, Marshall was also known as a writer who brought others alongside her as she tried to plumb the sometimes mysterious depths of prayer—and as a woman whose ministry brought together people who needed prayer and the strangers who volunteered to pray for them.

Adventures in Prayer, Marshall's slim volume on the subject, has sold more than a million copies since its 1975 publication. In it, and later in her prayer ministry, Marshall encouraged Christians to take seriously these words from James: "You do not have, because you do not ask" (James 4:2 NIV).

Thinking Too Little of God

The reason many of us retreat into vague generalities when we pray is not because we think too highly of God, but because we think too little," she wrote. "If we pray for something definite and our request is not granted, we fear to lose the little faith we had. So we fall back on the safe route of highly 'spiri-

> He is also able to save to the uttermost those who come to God through Him, since He always lives to make intercession for them.
>
> Hebrews 7:25 NKJV
>
> I urge, then, first of all, that requests, prayers, intercession and thanksgiving be made for everyone—for kings and all those in authority, that we may live peaceful and quiet lives in all godliness and holiness. This is good, and pleases God our Savior, who wants all men to be saved and to come to a knowledge of the truth.
>
> 1 Timothy 2:1–4 NIV

tual' prayers—the kind that Jesus brushed aside as not true prayer at all, just self-deceptive 'talking to ourselves.'"

During her childhood in Appalachia, Marshall learned the power of prayer from her mother, who refused to see poverty as an obstacle to Catherine's dream of attending college. They committed the matter to prayer, and soon after her mother received an unusual writing assignment that helped send Catherine to the college where she met her future husband, Peter Marshall, who later became U.S. Senate chaplain.

Anonymous Intercession

In 1980, three years before her death, Marshall launched Breakthrough, a ministry that distributes prayer requests anonymously to Christians who pray for twenty-one days and offer insights they receive during that time.

"Intercession is work," she said of the ministry. "It means caring about others as much as ourselves, as well as sacrificing our time."

Intercessory prayer is praying on behalf of others. The direct translation from its Latin roots is "to go between"; intercessors "go between" God and other people to pray in their place. The Bible provides numerous examples of intercessory prayer and reminds us of those we should be praying for.

Whom Are We to Pray For?

Pray for . . .	Scripture
All people	1 Timothy 2:1
Citizens of our country	Romans 10:1
Enemies	Jeremiah 29:7
Everyone who is in authority	1 Timothy 2:2
Friends	Job 42:8
Ministers of the gospel	Philippians 1:19
People of God	Psalm 122:6
People who abandon us	2 Timothy 4:16
Persecutors	Matthew 5:44
People who have health concerns	James 5:14

The Prayers of the Bible

Throughout the Bible, people of faith turned to God in their distress, in their need, in their joy. Many of their prayers reveal the cries of their hearts—and their expectation that God would respond.

Contents

Answer me when I call to you, O God who
declares me innocent. Free me from my troubles.
Have mercy on me and hear my prayer.

Psalm 4:1 NLT

Jesus' Prayer for All Believers—
How to Find Unity

It's been called the greatest prayer in the Bible—the words Jesus prayed in John 17 that have come to be known as the High Priestly Prayer. Of the approximately 650 prayers in the Bible, this prayer stands apart as Jesus' expression of love and concern for those who believe in him. In this prayer, Jesus' role as High Priest, which is thoroughly defined in the book of Hebrews, is evident. He continuously intercedes for the people of God. But instead of presenting a sacrifice to God, as the Jewish high priests did, he became the ultimate sacrifice.

The words of John 17 have offered comfort and assurance to Christians over the course of two millennia. But they've also caused many Christians to mourn the lack of unity in the church. After all, Jesus prayed not just that his followers would be "one," but also that their unity would mirror the oneness of the Trinity: "I am no longer in the world; and yet they themselves are in the world, and I come to You. Holy Father, keep them in Your name, the name which You have given Me, that they may be one even as We are" (John 17:11 NASB).

> Your love for one another will prove to the world that you are my disciples.
>
> John 13:35 NLT

> This is the kind of high priest we need: holy, innocent, undefiled, separated from sinners, and exalted above the heavens. He doesn't need to offer sacrifices every day, as high priests do—first for their own sins, then for those of the people. He did this once for all when He offered Himself.
>
> Hebrews 7:26–27 HCSB

Thousands of Denominations

Numerous sects claiming to be "Christian" existed following the resurrection, and even after the Roman Catholic and Orthodox churches unified believers to some extent, various smaller groups existed and at times flourished. But never in the past has the number of Christian denominations rivaled that which exists today. Depending on the method used to count and define denominations, the total may be as high as thirty-four thousand. Even the most conservative estimates top twenty thousand.

How does this square with Jesus' prayer for unity? Was Jesus' prayer ineffective? Did God not honor his Son's request? Jesus' plea is recorded several verses later: "I do not ask on behalf of these alone, but for those also who believe in Me through their word; that they may all be one; even as You, Father, are in Me and I in You, that they also may be in Us, so that the world may believe that You sent Me. The glory which You have given Me I have given to them, that they may be one, just as We are one; I in them and You in Me, that they may be perfected in unity, so that the world may know that You sent Me, and loved them, even as You have loved Me" (John 17:20–23 NASB).

Understanding of Unity

Jesus expanded the purpose of his request. He didn't want only for believers to experience the wonderful unity he and his Father shared; he also wanted their unity to testify to his identity as the Son of God. Many would say Christians have failed Jesus in this regard. It's hard to argue with those who point to denominations as evidence of Christians' disunity—unless unity is to be understood in a much broader sense.

Here's a major distinction to remember when the topic of Christian unity—or disunity—comes up: unity does not equal complete agreement. If it did, ministers would find it impossible to "unite" any couple in marriage. If you are married, or if you have observed your parents or other married couples, you know two spouses don't agree on everything. But they are still "one," according to the biblical definition of marriage (Genesis 2:24).

Think, too, of the unity found in the Trinity. The three persons of the Trinity are one, yet they have distinct roles. Their roles in no way interfere with their oneness.

But neither a lack of agreement in marriage nor the distinct roles in the Trinity justify the high number of denominations, especially those that disagree on basic doctrines. Two responses to this are the ecumenical movement, which seeks to unite certain Christian denominations, and the interfaith movement, which fosters respect for all faiths. Many Christians, however, are uncomfortable with those efforts and feel powerless to overcome denominationalism.

> I told my followers what you told me, and they accepted it. They know that I came from you, and they believe that you are the one who sent me. I am praying for them, but not for those who belong to this world. My followers belong to you, and I am praying for them.
>
> John 17:8–9 CEV

Unity Across Denominational Lines

Short of a genuine miracle, it's unlikely that denominations will ever disappear. But believers who trust in Christ are already one, regardless of denominational label. And many have found unity across denominational lines by praying together, thanking God for the unity they do have. When you focus on common ground, you begin to discover the unity that exists, often in surprising places.

Better yet, by dwelling in that place of common ground with other believers, you become something you probably thought you could never be: an answer to Jesus' High Priestly Prayer.

Throughout the New Testament, Jesus and the writers of the Epistles emphasized the need for love, respect, care, harmony, and peace among believers—in short, unity. Below are some of the many verses that encourage Christians to become one.

Scriptural Encouragement to Become One

Reason/Admonition for Unity	Scripture
Accept one another.	Romans 15:7
Be devoted to one another.	Acts 2:42-47
Be harmonious, brotherly.	1 Peter 3:8
Be like-minded and live in peace.	2 Corinthians 13:11
Be of the same mind, in one accord.	Romans 15:5-6
Be united in mind, love, spirit and purpose.	Philippians 2:1-4
Bear one another's burdens.	Galatians 6:1-2
Bear with one another and forgive each other.	Colossians 3:12-15
Encourage one another.	Hebrews 10:24-25
Give preference to one another.	Romans 12:10
God is a God of peace and not confusion.	1 Corinthians 14:33
God joins people together.	Mark 10:9
Have fellowship with one another.	1 John 1:7
Jesus and the church are bound together on earth and in heaven.	Matthew 18:15-18
Jesus established the church.	Matthew 16:18
Live in harmony.	Philippians 4:2
Live in peace with one another.	1 Thessalonians 5:13
Love one another.	John 13:34-35
Love one another with a pure heart.	1 Peter 1:22
Love the brotherhood.	1 Peter 2:17
Love your neighbor and fulfill the law.	Romans 13:8
Preserve the unity of the Spirit.	Ephesians 4:1-6
Pursue peace with one another.	Romans 14:19
We are members of one body.	1 Corinthians 12:12-31
We are one body in Christ.	Romans 12:4-5
We are one in Christ.	Galatians 3:28
Whole body is united.	Ephesians 4:16

Paul's Prayers for the Churches—
How to Grow in Faith

The apostle Paul is considered among the greatest spiritual writers in all of history, and for good reason. His letters to the people of the early church who were scattered throughout the Mediterranean area reveal the mind and heart of an educated wordsmith devoted to Jesus. Even many of his detractors admit that while they may not always like what he wrote, particularly about women's roles in the church, they recognize him as a brilliant communicator. And few passages from his letters surpass the expression of his mind and heart that he revealed in his prayers for the church.

A Man Who Used Talent from God

Upon Paul's conversion, God transformed the apostle's former zeal for persecuting the church into a passion for serving the church. Because the New Testament includes so many of Paul's writings, with thirteen letters attributed to him, today's believers have a clearer picture of who he was than they have of most of the other apostles. The picture that emerges is of a man who used the talent God gave him in service to the church. For Paul, that gift from God was one of communication.

In addition to communicating the gospel to the world around him,

God chose you, and we keep praying that God will make you worthy of being his people. We pray for God's power to help you do all the good things that you hope to do and that your faith makes you want to do.

2 Thessalonians 1:11 CEV

We always thank God, the Father of our Lord Jesus Christ, when we pray for you, for we have heard of your faith in Christ Jesus and of the love you have for all the saints because of the hope reserved for you in heaven. You have already heard about this hope in the message of truth.

Colossians 1:3–5 HCSB

Paul expressed his deepest longings for the church to God and to the church itself. Those longings frequently centered on his desire to see Christians grow in the faith, acquiring not only knowledge (fact-based information about the truth of God) but also wisdom (the life application of that knowledge of God): "I pray that the eyes of your heart may be enlightened, so that you will know what is the hope of His calling, what are the riches of the glory of His inheritance in the saints, and what is the surpassing greatness of His power toward us who believe" (Ephesians 1:18-19 NASB).

Knowing the Fullness of God

But even as he prayed for the church to grow in faith, Paul bowed his knees before God and prayed that the followers of Jesus would gain an even greater knowledge—a deeper understanding of the love of God.

Later, in his letter to the Ephesian church, he wrote that it was his prayer that believers would "be able to comprehend with all the saints what is the breadth and length and height and depth, and to know the love of Christ which surpasses knowledge, that you may be filled up to all the fullness of God" (Ephesians 3:18-19 NASB). Paul understood that even as he prayed for Christians to grasp the dimensions of Christ's love, the full magnitude of that love was beyond human comprehension. He wanted the followers of Christ to continually aim higher in their efforts to know God and his love.

In nearly all his prayers, Paul expressed his thankfulness to God for all who have come to Christ. Repeatedly in his epistles he assured the Christians to whom he was writing that he prayed for them without ceasing; Paul fully understood the persecution, temptations, and challenges they faced.

Broad Needs of the Church

Few people have the gift of eloquence that Paul had, but his prayers for the church can still serve as a model for Christians today. Throughout his epistles, Paul prayed at times for the more practical needs of the church, and those are not to be ignored. But there was also a place for prayer for the broader needs of the church—the need to get to know God, grow in faith, know the love of Christ, have the eyes of the heart enlightened, know the hope of his calling, and be filled with the fullness of God.

> This is my prayer: that your love may abound more and more in knowledge and depth of insight, so that you may be able to discern what is best and may be pure and blameless until the day of Christ, filled with the fruit of righteousness that comes through Jesus Christ—to the glory and praise of God.
>
> Philippians 1:9–11 NIV

Praying for healing, financial blessing, comfort, reconciliation, salvation, and so many other concerns is crucial to the faith and functioning of the body of Christ. Next time you pray about those needs, consider praying also for the church as a whole, the entire body of Christ. You can start by praying Paul's prayers for the church directly to God. Soon enough, you'll likely progress on to your own concerns for the universal church—and for all of the ways the church can continue to grow in order to become a powerful witness for Christ, an example to all of the "breadth and length and height and depth" of his love.

Digging Deeper

Paul prayed for the church throughout his letters, which are peppered with expressions of his hopes for believers. Here is a short list of his prayers:

• Prayer for endurance amid trouble (Colossians 1:9-14)

• Prayer for power to be strong in love and faith (Ephesians 3:14-21)

• Prayer for purity and wisdom to make right choices (Philippians 1:3-11)

• Prayer for the ability to do good works (2 Thessalonians 1:11-12)

- Prayer for wisdom, revelation and understanding of the truth (Ephesians 1:15-23)

- Prayer of thankfulness for the believers' hope in Christ (Colossians 1:3-6)

Check Your Understanding

- **Paul prayed that Christians would grow in both knowledge and wisdom. What is the difference between the two?**

In a Christian context, knowledge is information about God—who he is, what has been his plan of redemption throughout history, why Jesus came, what the Scriptures say. Wisdom is applying all of that knowledge to daily life.

- **Paul prayed such lofty prayers for believers, both in content and in style. How can his prayers serve as a model for others?**

Paul had a God-given talent for communication. His eloquence should never hinder Christians from praying. But the content of his prayers for the church is an example of how believers might want to pray.

- **Above all else, what did Paul want the church to have?**

Paul wanted believers to comprehend the measure of God's love for the church—and the power contained in that love to bring others to Christ.

Something to Ponder

God wants all Christians to share the gospel with others. But Paul's gift of communication can seem daunting to those who feel they don't have a way with words or may be introverted. If that's you, take a look at the gifts you do have and think about the ways God can use those gifts to help you share your faith with others.

Nehemiah's Prayer Project—
"Have Mercy and Answer My Prayer"

If you've ever been far from loved ones when catastrophe has struck, you know how helpless you can feel. You want to go and help, but for whatever reason, you can't leave where you are. Nehemiah found himself in just such a situation. News reached him in Persia that Jerusalem lay in ruins, and he left this record of his reaction: "When I heard this, I sat down and cried. Then for several days, I mourned; I went without eating to show my sorrow, and I prayed."

✳

Crying Out to God

Nehemiah's heart ached for the exiles who had returned to Jerusalem only to discover that the city had deteriorated into a pile of rubble. He cried out to God, but he didn't begin by making a request.

Instead, he affirmed his commitment and subservience to God, establishing his right to seek God's mercy and expect an answer to his constant prayers for the people of Israel (Nehemiah 1:6). He continued with a confession that is both personal and corporate; he and the Israelites had sinned by disobeying God and the law of Moses (v. 7). Only then did he make his petition, asking God to remember the promises he had made to the Israelites through Moses: "You told him that if we were unfaithful, you would scatter us among foreign nations. But you

> LORD God of heaven, you are great and fearsome. And you faithfully keep your promises to everyone who loves you and obeys your commands.
>
> Nehemiah 1:5 CEV
>
> Our LORD, I am praying for your servants—those you rescued by your great strength and mighty power. Please answer my prayer and the prayer of your other servants who gladly honor your name.
>
> Nehemiah 1:10–11 CEV

also said that no matter how far away we were, we could turn to you and start obeying your laws. Then you would bring us back to the place where you have chosen to be worshiped" (Nehemiah 1:8–9 CEV).

Pleading for God's Mercy

Notice how he prayed. As a servant of God, he pleaded for God's mercy and for answers to his prayers. He confessed the sins of his family, himself, and the people of God, and he reminded God of his promises.

Nehemiah did what he could do: He asked. He confessed. He reminded. When you feel helpless, remember Nehemiah. From a distance, he cried and he fasted, but he also prayed. And God was faithful to answer; the king granted him permission to return to Jerusalem to help the people of God rebuild the city.

Digging Deeper

As cupbearer to the Persian king, Nehemiah held a position of great responsibility. The position not only involved preventing the king from being intentionally or accidentally poisoned but also serving as a trusted adviser, similar to a prime minister. Nehemiah was the third man in Jewish history to serve as cupbearer to a foreign king; Joseph held the position of cupbearer in Egypt, while Daniel did the same in Babylon.

Final Thoughts

Nehemiah's sorrow was evident. When King Artaxerxes asked why he was sad, Nehemiah feared that if his answer displeased the king, he could lose his life. He prayed, and he related his desire to rebuild Jerusalem. Instead of beheading him, Artaxerxes asked him to make his request specific: How long would he be gone? When did he expect to return? As a servant of God, he had nothing to fear.

Hannah's Heart—"He's My Child"

For years, Hannah suffered the derision of Peninnah, her husband's other wife, during their journeys from their hometown of Ramah to Shiloh to observe the annual religious feasts. Peninnah, the mother of Elkanah's children, was well aware of Elkanah's preference for Hannah. Out of jealousy, she taunted Hannah because she was childless. One year, Hannah could not take Peninnah's torment any longer. She finished her meal and ran to the tabernacle, where the high priest Eli observed her behavior—and accused her of drunkenness.

Hannah in Anguish

But Hannah was pouring out her anguish to God: "LORD All-Powerful, I am your servant, but I am so miserable! Please let me have a son. I will give him to you for as long as he lives, and his hair will never be cut" (1 Samuel 1:11 CEV).

Eli could see her lips move, but no sound came out of her mouth. He assumed she was drunk. Hannah denied that and explained her sorrow: "'Sir, please don't think I'm no good!' Hannah answered. 'I'm not drunk, and I haven't been drinking. But I do feel miserable and terribly upset. I've been praying all this time, telling the LORD about my problems.' Eli replied, 'You may go home now and stop worrying. I'm sure the God of Israel will answer your prayer'" (1 Samuel 1:15–17 CEV).

Peninnah liked to make Hannah feel miserable about not having any children, especially when the family went to the house of the LORD each year. One day, Elkanah was there offering a sacrifice, when Hannah began crying and refused to eat. So Elkanah asked, "Hannah, why are you crying? Why won't you eat? Why do you feel so bad? Don't I mean more to you than ten sons?"

1 Samuel 1:6–8 CEV

God Honored Prayer

God honored Hannah's prayer and Eli's blessing. In due time, she gave birth to a son—Samuel, who would be the last judge of the Israelites. As she promised, Hannah gave Samuel to God; when he was three, she took him to live with and learn from Eli.

Leaving Samuel behind must have been difficult. But instead of mourning, Hannah praised God for his goodness: "You make me strong and happy, Lord. You rescued me. Now I can be glad and laugh at my enemies" (1 Samuel 2:1 CEV).

Hannah's song of thanksgiving lives on in Scripture—a tribute to a woman who trusted God completely and fulfilled her vow to him.

Digging Deeper

Hannah vowed that no razor would be used on her future son's head (1 Samuel 1:11). This refers to the Nazirite vow, through which a man was consecrated to God. Nazirites could not consume wine, beer, vinegar made from either beverage, or any product of a grapevine (grapes, raisins). They also could not cut their hair; thus, no razor would be used on their heads. Both Samson and John the Baptist were Nazirites.

Something to Ponder

In Israelite society, a barren woman was a scorned woman. Conceiving and giving birth to Samuel was undoubtedly the high point of Hannah's life. But she had made a vow to God, which was a serious act; no honorable person would break such a vow. Think about what you would do if you made a difficult vow and then had to make good on it.

Elijah's Prayer—"God, Reveal Yourself to Me"

The people of God had been led into error, leaving the one true God in favor of worshipping an idol—Baal. Only one prophet of God remained. But if you can have only one prophet, you would want a prophet like the one who survived: Elijah the Tishbite. Elijah confronted the people with a challenge: he would pit his God against any other any day. It was time for a showdown. If God won the challenge, the people would follow him; if Baal won, the people would follow him. Elijah, the lone prophet of God, prepared to face the prophets of Baal—all 450 of them.

✳

The Prophets of Baal

The rules were these: both Elijah and the Baal prophets would slaughter an ox, place it on a wooden altar, and pray for their respective deities to ignite the fire. Elijah let his opposition go first. The prophets of Baal prayed all morning long and began jumping on the altar, but nothing happened.

"About noontime Elijah began mocking them. 'You'll have to shout louder,' he scoffed, 'for surely he is a god! Perhaps he is daydreaming, or is relieving himself. Or maybe he is away on a trip, or is asleep and needs to be wakened!'" (1 Kings 18:27 NLT). This enraged the prophets further, and they began praying louder and cutting themselves as part of a religious ritual.

Elijah was a man with a nature like ours, and he prayed earnestly that it would not rain, and it did not rain on the earth for three years and six months.

James 5:17 NASB

Jesus took Peter, James, and John and led them up a high mountain. His appearance changed from the inside out, right before their eyes. His clothes shimmered, glistening white, whiter than any bleach could make them. Elijah, along with Moses, came into view, in deep conversation with Jesus.

Mark 9:2–4 MSG

Elijah's Prayer to the True God

Elijah had enough and called an end to the prophets' petitions. He rebuilt the altar, placed his slaughtered ox on it—and drenched the whole works with bucket after bucket of water. And then he prayed: "O GOD, God of Abraham, Isaac, and Israel, make it known right now that you are God in Israel, that I am your servant, and that I'm doing what I'm doing under your orders. Answer me, GOD; O answer me and reveal to this people that you are GOD, the true God, and that you are giving these people another chance at repentance" (1 Kings 18:36–37 MSG).

The result? The people believed what was right before their eyes, the evidence that there is only one true God—and his name is not Baal.

Digging Deeper

 When Elijah rebuilt the altar that had proved to be a failure for the prophets of Baal, he performed a symbolic gesture on behalf of the nation of Israel. After gathering twelve stones, he placed them in the wood on the altar. The stones represented the twelve tribes of Israel, and Elijah's gesture was his way of showing honor to God.

Check Your Understanding

- **Why did Elijah challenge the prophets of Baal?**

The Israelites had been enticed into worshipping Baal. The burden of returning them to God fell to Elijah, the last remaining prophet. So sure was his faith in God that he issued the challenge to prove that there was only one powerful God.

- **How did Elijah give the prophets of Baal an advantage?**

Elijah drenched the altar with water to make the challenge more difficult. Baal's prophets had already lost, but Elijah would not have won; a stalemate would have resulted. But God proved himself to be all-powerful.

David's Prayer of Protection—"Hide Me"

The book of Psalms is among the best known and most loved in all of Scripture. The poetry is often of the highest quality, but the cry of the human heart found in the individual psalms sets the poems apart as expressions of a deep hunger for God. The poems, prayers, and songs of praise found in this book cover the spectrum of human need. And because he was so relentlessly pursued by so many enemies, the psalmist David often called out to God to meet one need in particular: the need for protection.

✳

David's Images of God's Protection

When it came to describing the way God defended him, David abandoned the abstract in favor of visual imagery. When he needed God's protection, David saw God as a shield, a fortress, a refuge, a shelter, a high and strong tower—even as wings. In Psalm 57, that's the protection he sought when his archenemy, Saul, entered the cave David was hiding in: "God Most High, have pity on me! Have mercy. I run to you for safety. In the shadow of your wings, I seek protection till danger dies down" (v. 1 CEV).

Even though he had sought refuge in a cave, David needed more than mere limestone to protect him. He needed the shadow of God's wings—a comforting image for you to carry with you and call upon whenever you are fearful or exposed to danger.

> In the time of trouble He shall hide me in His pavilion; in the secret place of His tabernacle He shall hide me; He shall set me high upon a rock.
>
> Psalm 27:5 NKJV

> You're my cave to hide in, my cliff to climb. Be my safe leader, be my true mountain guide. Free me from hidden traps; I want to hide in you. I've put my life in your hands. You won't drop me, you'll never let me down.
>
> Psalm 31:3–5 MSG

Power of David's Words

David also sought protection from danger of a different kind: "Hide me from the conspiracy of the wicked, from that noisy crowd of evildoers. They sharpen their tongues like swords and aim their words like deadly arrows " (Psalm 64:2-3 NIV). David the poet was well aware of the power of words—and the power of God to "turn their own tongues against them and bring them to ruin; all who see them will shake their heads in scorn" (Psalm 64:8 NIV).

Whatever you need protection from, God is there to hide you from your enemies—whether as a mighty fortress or as a wing-shaped shadow.

In the psalms and elsewhere, biblical writers used imagery to convey the way they visualized God's protection.

God as a Refuge

Kind of Refuge	Scripture
Fortress	2 Samuel 22:2-3 Psalms 59; 94
Hiding place	Psalms 32; 119
Refuge	Deuteronomy 33:27 Psalms 11; 31; 46; 62; 67; 118 Proverbs 14 Isaiah 25 Hebrews 6
Shelter	Psalm 27
Shield	Genesis 15 Psalms 3; 18; 28 2 Corinthians 2 Ephesians 6
Wings	Psalms 17; 57; 91

Solomon's Humility—"Grant Me Wisdom"

What is the first quality that comes to mind when you hear the name of Solomon? Most likely, it's wisdom. Solomon's request that God grant him wisdom to rule Israel is known even among those who have little knowledge of the rest of the Bible. The "wisdom of Solomon" is legendary. The irony, of course, is that Solomon even thought he had to ask for wisdom—because Solomon already had the wisdom to ask for wisdom.

✳

Conflicts on a Number of Fronts

Solomon was a son of David who had been appointed king over Israel as David lay dying. As he assumed his royal position, he faced conflict on a number of fronts. He faced opposition from two factions that believed someone else should be king: the followers of the high priest Abiathar, who had been deposed; and the followers of Solomon's brother Adonijah, who was later executed. Solomon knew both factions would continue to cause unrest once he ascended to the throne.

Solomon's request for wisdom came in response to a question God asked him in a dream after he became king: "What can I give you?"

> Nothing is its equal—not gold or costly glass. Wisdom is worth much more than coral, jasper, or rubies. All the topaz of Ethiopia and the finest gold cannot compare with it.
>
> Job 28:17–19 CEV

> The fear of the LORD is the beginning of wisdom; a good understanding have all those who do His commandments. His praise endures forever.
>
> Psalm 111:10 NKJV

Youthful Inexperience

After recounting God's love and faithfulness to his father, David, Solomon admitted to his youthful inexperience in light of the enormous task of reigning over the nation of Israel, a nation so large that its population was too high to record (1 Kings 3:7-8). Only then does he make his request: "Give Your servant an obedient heart to judge Your people and to discern between good and evil. For who is able to judge this great people of Yours?" (1 Kings 3:9 HCSB).

Bear in mind that Solomon was all of twenty years old when he became

king. Solomon's request revealed another quality: humility. His humble request reveals his insecurity over whether he was mature enough to be equipped to discern between good and evil.

Solomon's response was pleasing to God, who pointed out all the things Solomon could have asked for: a long life, personal wealth, revenge against his enemies— who were already threatening his kingdom. But because he considered the welfare of God's people above his own desires, God rewarded him by promising to give him much more than he requested.

Wisdom, Understanding, Wealth, and Honor

God not only gave Solomon wisdom and understanding; he also showered him with wealth and honor and a singular place in history (1 Kings 3:11-13). Not only would there never be another person like Solomon, but God assured him there would be no other king like him as long as he lived.

Humility is always pleasing to God. Praying with humility shows an acknowledgment of God's sovereignty; when you humble yourself before God, you own up to your position of subservience. A humble heart recognizes God as Lord, and such a heart is rewarded: "The LORD takes pleasure in His people; He adorns the humble with salvation" (Psalm 149:4 HCSB).

Solomon's Reward

After promising Solomon riches and honor, God rewarded him for his humble request:

• Solomon ruled over an enormous kingdom, from Egypt to the Euphrates.

• During his lifetime, peace reigned throughout his kingdom; the borders were kept safe.

• Every family in his kingdom enjoyed security and some measure of prosperity.

• Solomon's prosperity was unrivaled in the known world.

• His fame was known among the surrounding nations; ambassadors came from far and wide to partake of his wisdom.

• His intellect was also legendary; he was well-versed in both botany and zoology, and was a prolific writer, composing three thousand proverbs and more than one thousand songs.

> Keep in tune with wisdom and think what it means to have common sense. Beg as loud as you can for good common sense. Search for wisdom as you would search for silver or hidden treasure.
>
> Proverbs 2:2–4 CEV

And the wisdom God promised him? Solomon became known throughout the region for his wisdom, knowledge, and understanding; 1 Kings 4:29–31 indicates that his wisdom was greater than that of all the wisdom teachers from Babylon to Egypt, including some of such renown that their names were recorded in the Bible.

Indeed, no other king was like him as long as he lived, just as God had assured him. By humbling himself, acknowledging his shortcomings, and asking God to give him a heart willing to listen to the voice of God, Solomon received far more than he asked for—and nearly everyone under his authority benefited.

Digging Deeper

One of the greatest of Solomon's achievements was construction of the temple. Though many attempts have been made to create an accurate model of the temple based on biblical dimensions, the unit of measure, the cubit, represented different lengths in different cultures. Regardless of its size, it is generally agreed that gold played a prominent role, with an estimated twenty tons used in its construction. In addition, King Solomon received an annual revenue in excess of $256 million in gold over a period of forty years.

Points to Remember

• God chooses the way he communicates; he spoke to Solomon in a dream.

• Solomon humbled himself before God.

• Acknowledging his inexperience, he asked for a heart willing to listen to God's wisdom.

• Solomon's request pleased God, who promised more than he asked for.

• Humility indicates an attitude of respectful subservience to God.

Final Thoughts

Despite his auspicious beginning, Solomon's later years were marked by moral failure. With some seven hundred women in his life, he became distracted and abandoned the things of God. In fact, he began worshipping other gods. His wealth and power had taken its toll. God had promised him a long life if only he would serve him with his whole heart. Solomon, who was sixty when he died, did not live a particularly long life.

Jude's Praise—Worshipping Through Prayer

Every week in liturgical churches, those that follow a formal ritual, the congregation sings or chants a particular form of praise to God. Among the most familiar are the Gloria Patri ("Glory Be to the Father") and the Doxology ("Praise God from Whom All Blessings Flow"). Less familiar is the doxology found at the end of the epistle of Jude, a letter possibly written by a brother of Jesus and intended to be circulated among all the churches. What sets Jude's doxology apart is the context in which it was written.

✣

Unique Among New Testament Letters

Jude's brief letter consisting of just twenty-five verses is unique among New Testament letters not only for its brevity but also for its harsh tone. Jude begins on a note of regret; he had wanted to write about their shared salvation, presumably a more uplifting topic, but he felt led to issue a warning instead. Evildoers guilty of sexual sin had infiltrated the church.

Jude minced no words in describing these wicked people: they had "given themselves over to sexual immorality" (Jude 7 NKJV), rejected authority, and spoken evil of things they knew nothing about. Moreover, they were a blemish on the communal meals that Christians shared, sinners who were "twice dead . . . foaming up their own shame" (Jude 12–13 NKJV), who lived by their lust, and who caused division in the church.

> Keep building on the foundation of your most holy faith, as the Holy Spirit helps you to pray. And keep in step with God's love, as you wait for our Lord Jesus Christ to show how kind he is by giving you eternal life. Be helpful to all who may have doubts.
>
> Jude 20–22 CEV

Troublemakers in Their Midst

Jude left little doubt how he felt about the troublemakers in their midst.

But then, when he reached the end of his diatribe, Jude remembered the one who makes everything right, and he broke out into praise: "To Him who is able to keep you from stumbling, and to present you faultless before the presence of His glory with exceeding joy, to God our Savior, who alone is wise, be glory and majesty, dominion and power, both now and forever. Amen" (Jude 24-25 NKJV).

Jude left the matter of the infiltrators where it belonged: in the hands of the only wise God, who alone could keep those under Jude's care pure and blameless.

Digging Deeper

Biblical writers who railed against the wicked frequently ended on a note of praise or humility; you can almost hear a sigh of relief when their thoughts turned toward God. In Psalm 139, for example, after writing an eloquent and memorable poem about God, David suddenly expressed his hatred for the wicked. But he ended by turning back to God: "Look deep into my heart, God, and find out everything I am thinking. Don't let me follow evil ways, but lead me in the way that time has proven true" (vv. 23-24 CEV). As you read through the psalms, note how often the writers did this.

Final Thoughts

Jude reminded Christians that God is able to keep them from "stumbling," which means much more than simply getting tripped up by sin now and then. It means falling away from the faith completely. Jude's choice of words was no coincidence. After issuing a stern warning about former believers wreaking havoc on the church, Jude underscored the importance of relying on God to keep your life and faith pure.

Stephen's Final Prayer—
What to Pray at Life's End

It isn't unusual for the dying to have visions or to cry out to God with their last breath. What is unusual is for a dying person to see the heavens open or to see the Son of Man standing at the right hand of God. Stephen saw both. But as dramatic as that was, that vision didn't provide the only extraordinary moment as he neared death. A second striking event occurred when Stephen cried out to God, with his last breath, to forgive the very people responsible for his death.

✤

Remarkable Spiritual Gifts

Stephen was among seven apostles chosen to distribute food to the widows among the Christians in Jerusalem. That may not sound like an important job, but the seven were chosen precisely because of their remarkable spiritual gifts. The widows needed their wisdom and compassion.

Stephen also distinguished himself by performing "signs and wonders," which attracted crowds and the attention of the synagogue leaders. The leaders leveled numerous accusations against him, started rumors about him, and tried to turn the people against him. Eventually Stephen was brought up on charges of blasphemy.

God gave Stephen the power to work great miracles and wonders among the people. But some Jews from Cyrene and Alexandria were members of a group who called themselves "Free Men." They started arguing with Stephen. Some others from Cilicia and Asia also argued with him. But they were no match for Stephen, who spoke with the great wisdom that the Spirit gave him. So they talked some men into saying, "We heard Stephen say terrible things against Moses and God!"

Acts 6:8–11 CEV

Jude's Accusation

At his trial, Stephen stood before the religious council and began preaching about God's plan of redemption. He finished with an accusation: "You stubborn people! You are heathen at heart and deaf to the truth. Must you forever resist the Holy Spirit? That's what your ancestors did, and so do you! Name one prophet your ancestors didn't persecute! They even killed the ones who predicted the coming of the Righteous One—the Messiah whom you betrayed and murdered" (Acts 7:51-52 NLT).

At that, the Jewish leaders became enraged. They rushed at him, dragged him outside the city, and began stoning him. Among the angry crowd that day was Saul of Tarsus, who would need the forgiveness Stephen prayed about.

Something to Ponder

There are times when forgiveness seems to be in short supply, and at other times tragic events—such as the schoolhouse massacre of Amish children in 2006—are marked by an outpouring of forgiveness. Experts in the field say forgiveness needs to be practiced on a daily basis so it becomes an automatic but genuine response when it is most needed. How can you practice forgiveness in your everyday life?

Digging Deeper

Stephen's trial proved to be a turning point in the history of the fledgling church. The Jewish leaders ramped up their persecution of the Christians, and soon only the apostles were left in Jerusalem. But as the persecuted Christians fled to the surrounding countryside, they took with them the good news about Jesus Christ.  The stoning of Stephen, the church's first martyr, was the catalyst that caused the gospel to be spread far beyond Jerusalem.

Praying in the Middle of Life for You and Others

In some situations, it's hard to know how to pray with intelligence and wisdom. Circumstances can seem so overwhelming at times that it helps to have guidance on how to pray.

Contents

In certain ways we are weak, but the Spirit is here to help us. For example, when we don't know what to pray for, the Spirit prays for us in ways that cannot be put into words. All of our thoughts are known to God. He can understand what is in the mind of the Spirit, as the Spirit prays for God's people.

Romans 8:26–27 CEV

How to Pray with Joy When Money Is Tight and a Baby Is on the Way

The addition of a baby to any family is always an occasion for celebration, right? Babies are the best kind of people in the whole world. Who wouldn't be joyful when a baby arrives? Praying about that would be a piece of cake. Not so fast. The arrival of a new baby should be cause for celebration. But money is tight; you're down to one paycheck, and that source of income is no longer secure. How can you pray with joy when the situation is so uncertain?

✳

As a Christian, you believe life is sacred and children are a blessing from God. You also believe that having a child is a serious responsibility. The child's life is in your hands, and you need to be able to meet your baby's most basic needs. But right now, you can barely meet the needs of your other children. How can you provide for another one?

Financial Worries

Financial worries can rob you of joy in every area of your life—and even more so when a little one is on the way, whether through birth or adoption. Because the arrival of a baby is usually such a joyous occasion, when that joy is taken from you, the emotional swing is acute. When a situation that was once so full of hope changes dramatically, fear doesn't creep in; it lands on you with a thud.

> Some people were even bringing infants to Him so He might touch them, but when the disciples saw it, they rebuked them. Jesus, however, invited them: "Let the little children come to Me, and don't stop them, because the kingdom of God belongs to such as these."
>
> Luke 18:15–16 HCSB

> Children are a gift from the LORD; they are a reward from him.
>
> Psalm 127:3 NLT

One way to rediscover that joy is to identify your specific fears and uncertainties. You likely have immediate concerns, like medical costs,  and long-range concerns about caring for a child for the next two decades. The latter is fueled by dismal reports about the cost of rearing a child from birth to age eighteen, which the U.S. Department of Agriculture estimates to be more than $190,000. Numbers like that can be dizzying to expectant parents, but they are also unrealistic. You have the wisdom of God at your disposal, which means you are much less likely to be as indulgent as that exorbitant figure would indicate.

Start with Prayer

But you still have those immediate worries. You may feel as if there's not much you can do before the baby arrives, but preparing financially for a baby begins the moment you learn a child is on the way (if you're expecting an adopted child, you are already well aware of this!). There's actually a great deal you can do, starting with praying some very specific prayers:

- Thank God for providing for all your needs (Philippians 4:19).

- Acknowledge that children are a blessing from God (Psalm 123:7).

- Ask God to restore the joy of your salvation (Psalm 51:12).

- Pray for the child that God is forming in the mother's womb (Psalm 139:13).

- Ask God to give you wisdom regarding your finances and other resources (James 1:5).

Remember, too, that you are blessed to live in a time when there's no need to reinvent the wheel. Lots of struggling couples have gone before you, and many are willing to share their experiences for free through online newsletters, blogs, and Web sites. Still others are professional money managers who specialize in helping families stay afloat in difficult times by offering books and other media that provide tips on saving and reusing and recycling the resources you already have.

Useful Advice and Practical Help

Best of all are the Christian parents you know who are generous with both useful advice and practical help. Many have raised large families on a shoestring without feeling deprived. In fact, many have discovered that the joy of having children—and lots of them!—far outweighs whatever they had to sacrifice to provide for their children. They will tell you that a bag of hand-me-downs brings them greater pleasure than a monthly subscription to a movie rental service and that one homemade meal provided by an empathetic friend is worth far more to them than a week of fast food.

> For this child I prayed, and the LORD has granted me my petition which I asked of Him.
>
> 1 Samuel 1:27 NKJV

Faith and action go hand in hand when times are tough and you have another child to care for. Believe that God will provide, but don't ignore the provision he has already made for you. Rely on God—and on the wisdom and practical help he wants other people to give you.

Throughout the tough times, don't forget to fully embrace the joy that comes with each new addition to your family. Children retain fond memories of the simple pleasures of life—playing outside, having stories read to them, going for a walk with Mom or Dad. By spending time with your children, you give them much more than your bank balance can ever provide.

It should help ease your long-term fears about the cost of rearing a child to look at the breakdown of projected costs (see page 194), some of which are far higher than a typical family would spend. Without sacrificing the quality of care you provide, you can easily reduce many of these costs by 50 percent—and some by 75 percent or more.

Projected Costs of Rearing a Child

Expense	Age Range	Cost per Year	Multiply by No. of Years	Total
Child care	0–11	4,300	11 years	47,300
Groceries	0–18	1,525	18 years	27,450
Clothing	0–18	606	18 years	10,908
Gift giving	0–18	330	18 years	5,940
Bigger home	0–18	2,900	18 years	52,200
Bigger car	5–18	1,250	13 years	16,250
Education	5–18	600	13 years	7,800
Recreation	0–18	330	18 years	5,940
Added insurance	0–18	300	18 years	5,400
Health care	0–18	300	18 years	5,400
Miscellaneous	0–18	330	18 years	5,940
TOTAL		$12,771		$190,528

*Projected costs are based on national averages; the amounts will change based on the region of the country in which you live. From information provided by USDA Publication 1528–2007 and Bankrate.com.

How to Pray with Longing While Trying to Discover God's Will

Should you accept that job offer? What's the best way to help your daughter decide which college to attend? Does God really want you to serve on the worship team when you're already overextended? These and similar questions send Christians on a relentless pursuit to discover God's will for their lives. Sometimes the questions apply to everyday matters, sometimes to life-changing decisions, and sometimes to big-picture scenarios like God's purpose for putting you on earth.

And sometimes, the best way to find out what you don't know is to figure out what you do know.

✢

What do you already know about God's will? You know that

- God has plans for a hopeful future for you (Jeremiah 29:11).

- God wants you to understand his will (Ephesians 5:17).

- Your plans need to take second place to God's (James 4:13-17).

- His will is good, acceptable, and perfect (Romans 12:2).

- His will is for everyone to come to salvation and knowledge of the truth (1 Timothy 2:3-4).

- If you ask for anything according to his will, God will hear you (1 John 5:14).

- If you do what you already know of God's will, his love is in you (1 John 2:4-5).

> Teach me to do your will, for you are my God. May your gracious Spirit lead me forward on a firm footing.
>
> Psalm 143:10 NLT

> Trust GOD from the bottom of your heart; don't try to figure out everything on your own. Listen for GOD's voice in everything you do, everywhere you go; he's the one who will keep you on track.
>
> Proverbs 3:5–6 MSG

God Wants to Reveal His Will

You probably know even more than that about God's will, but this is a good start. Looking over that list should give you the confidence of knowing that God wants to reveal his will to you. Pay special attention to the last item, because if you're not already doing what you know to be God's will—his revealed will in the pages of Scripture—it would be a good idea to start there. Christians who want to know God's specific will but aren't following God's will as revealed in the Bible have it all backward; they need to start following what they know—love God, love your neighbor, and other equally clear command-ments—before they ask him to fill them in on what they don't know.

Praying the Scriptures

Praying the Bible back to God is a great way to talk to God about anything in your life that you're uncertain about. Whenever you're seeking God's will for a specific situation, try this method of praying. Here are some examples:

"God, I need your wisdom for this situation. James 1:5 says that you will be generous with your wisdom if I ask for it. I believe the Bible, and I'm asking for wisdom now."

"God, I'm trusting you with all my heart. I'm not relying on my own understanding. You said in John 16:13 that if I acknowledge you in everything that I do, you will show me the way to go. I need to hear your voice. I need you to guide me toward the truth in this situation."

"God, you say in Proverbs 12:15 that a person who is wise will seek the counsel of others and listen to their advice. I need to know your will for my life, and I'm trusting you to speak to me through the people I trust to give me direction."

There's no lack of passages in Scripture that you can pray back to God. If you search the Bible, you will no doubt find many verses that express the longing of your heart to know God's will. Praying in this way assures you that you are praying in God's will as you pray for God's will.

Relax and Wait

During this time of seeking, it's important that you relax and wait on God. It's tempting to want to rush things and try to determine God's will right away. But as you've probably already learned, God is seldom in as much of a hurry as you are. Relaxing is tough when you have a deadline—you have until next week, say, to let a prospective employer know whether you'll take the job—but it's in those situations that you discover the depth of your trust in God.

> "I know the plans I have for you," says the LORD. "They are plans for good and not for disaster, to give you a future and a hope."
>
> Jeremiah 29:11 NLT

God's guidance for your problem may not always be as spelled-out as you might want. Be alert to your intuition, however. That is often God's will making itself known to you. Have you ever had the experience of sitting down to write a check or make an offer and had a number pop into your head? Have you ever "known" something without thinking about it? Oftentimes that is God talking to you. Does God say yes or no to the new job? You may already know.

Don't forget to thank God for revealing his will to you. Thanking God in advance, before you have the slightest inkling of what his will is, shows that you are praying with anticipation and the expectation that he will answer you.

The Bible offers lots of advice on how to determine God's specific will for your life. Following are some passages that will help you as you pray to know what God has in store for you.

How to Determine God's Will

God's Will for You	Scripture
Be courageous once you're sure of God's will.	Joshua 1:5-7
Be faithful with what you have now.	Luke 16:10
The Bible helps you to know his will.	Psalm 119:105
Do what you know; wait on the rest.	John 16:12
God has a plan for your life.	Jeremiah 29:11
God has given you gifts to use to do his will.	Ephesians 4:11-13
God wants you to advance the kingdom.	Philippians 1:2
God wants you to come to a saving knowledge of him.	1 Timothy 2:3-4
God will give you wisdom.	James 1:5
God will reveal his will if you are willing to follow it.	John 7:17
God will see your good work through to completion.	Philippians 1:6
God will speak to you in a still, small voice.	1 Kings 19:11-12
God will tell you which way you should go.	Isaiah 30:20-21
God's will for you is always in harmony with his Word.	Isaiah 8:20
God's will is perfect.	Romans 12:2
Heed the words of many advisers.	Proverbs 15:22
The Holy Spirit will guide you into all truth.	John 16:13
Jesus came to do God's will; follow his lead.	John 6:38
Listen to the advice of wise counsel.	Proverbs 12:15
Seek the advice of a multitude of counselors.	Proverbs 11:14
You can ask for anything.	Philippians 4:6
You can trust God to show you the way.	Proverbs 3:5-6
You must be fully committed to him.	Luke 9:23
You will have a sense of peace when you're in God's will.	Isaiah 32:17-18
Your purpose is to glorify him.	1 Corinthians 10:31

How to Pray with Wisdom in the Midst of Peer Pressure

Peer pressure knows no age limit. Parents who warn their teenagers about the dangers of going along with the crowd can sometimes be blind to their own concessions to the pressure exerted by their friends and coworkers. Resisting that pressure can be tricky for adults. Adults may sometimes be more aware of the pressure, but they're also more aware of the diplomacy involved in opposing it. Refusing to go along with a crowd of adults can have significant consequences.

✳

Consequences of going along with the crowd include being passed over for a promotion at work or losing your job entirely. That doesn't happen only in the business world; many a pastor has been seen to the door for standing on biblical ground in opposition to a long-standing unbiblical practice in a given congregation.

Unspoken Peer Pressure

Then there's the other kind of peer pressure: the unspoken, insidious type that compels you to go into debt to buy a luxury hybrid when the sedan you already own outright is perfectly fine.

> Do not be conformed to this age, but be transformed by the renewing of your mind, so that you may discern what is the good, pleasing, and perfect will of God.
>
> Romans 12:2 HCSB
>
> The one who walks with the wise will become wise, but a companion of fools will suffer harm.
>
> Proverbs 13:20 HCSB

Refusing to conform or compromise is difficult at any age. But it's especially important for adults to meet that challenge because so much is at stake; the next generation is looking to you as a role model, your own children are learning how to navigate adulthood from you, and there's the matter of your personal integrity.

The Perfect Antidote

The Bible offers the perfect antidote to peer pressure: transformation. And transformation comes by the renewing of your mind. Saturating your mind with wisdom from the Bible gives your life a spiritual makeover. Prayer plays a pivotal role in this transformation by strengthening your faith and opening you up to a greater understanding of the Word of God.

Something to Ponder

Peer pressure is usually spoken of in negative terms. But think about the many ways in which a group of your adult peers has influenced you in a positive way. In a sense, every culture and subculture is a reflection of the dominant mind-set of its adult population. Your church is likely an example of a subculture that has been "peer pressured" in a positive way.

Myth Buster

Because teenagers are under so much pressure to conform to their social group, it's assumed they're the only group subject to peer pressure. But adults are subject to it as well—and to a great extent. Here are some examples of adult peer pressure:

- Networking after-hours because it is essential to your job security
- Being a stay-at-home mother in a neighborhood of working mothers— or a working mother in a neighborhood of stay-at-home mothers
- Parishioners feeling forced to conform politically
- Keeping up appearances when you can no longer afford to
- Taking risky shortcuts to save the company money
- Buying things for your children they think they absolutely must have

How to Pray with Determination During Suffering or Persecution

Even those who know little about the Bible are often familiar with the story of Job, the man whose faith was tested after he lost his entire family and all his possessions. Not surprisingly, Job's name has become synonymous with suffering. Far fewer people are familiar with the story of David and Nancy Guthrie, although their story was compelling enough to warrant coverage by several major news outlets. To many who know what happened to the Guthries, their name has become synonymous with modern-day suffering.

The chances that the Guthries would suffer as they did are actually measurable. Zellweger syndrome is a disorder for which there is no treatment or cure. David and Nancy both carry a recessive gene for Zellweger syndrome, and the odds of that are 1 in 100,000. They learned that they both had it a few days after the birth of their second child, Hope. Just over six months later, Hope died. David got a vasectomy; Nancy conceived anyway, a 1 in 2,000 probability. This baby was also born with Zellweger's. Gabriel lived just under six months.

> Blessed are those who are persecuted because of righteousness, for theirs is the kingdom of heaven. Blessed are you when people insult you, persecute you and falsely say all kinds of evil against you because of me. Rejoice and be glad, because great is your reward in heaven, for in the same way they persecuted the prophets who were before you.
>
> Matthew 5:10–12 NIV

Suffering Serves a Purpose

At one time, people might have believed the Guthries were being punished for their sins. Most Christians today agree that suffering serves a purpose. That purpose may not be known this side of heaven, however, and bearing up under the weight of agonizing pain—physical, emotional, mental, spiritual—requires more than the promise of an unknown purpose.

Suffering Christians through the centuries have found comfort by viewing their pain in light of the cross—a symbol of suffering that led to a resurrected life. By sharing in the suffering of Christ, their pain became a pathway to a new life.

Contrary to conventional wisdom, the Bible frequently points out the benefits and rewards for those who endure suffering and persecution, particularly those who suffer for their faith.

Suffering, Persecution, and Endurance

Benefits/Rewards of Suffering	Scripture
Affliction is preparation for heaven.	2 Corinthians 4:17-18
Enduring pain for the gospel pleases God.	1 Peter 2:19-20
God's people are tested through suffering.	Psalm 66:10
Good can come from suffering.	Psalm 119:65-72
Hardship refines faith.	1 Peter 1:7
Jesus helps people through suffering.	Matthew 11:28-30
Jesus helps people through trials.	Hebrews 2:5-18
Pain yields righteousness.	Hebrews 12:11
Paul's suffering was foretold.	Acts 9:15-16
Persecution is inevitable.	John 16:33
Persecution leads to reward.	Matthew 5:10-12
Rejoicing amid trials leads to maturity.	James 1:2-4
Suffering brings blessing.	1 Peter 3:14
Suffering for Christ is a privilege.	Philippians 1:29
Suffering is to be expected.	1 Peter 4:12-14
Suffering reveals truth.	Isaiah 53:11
Suffering teaches humility.	Deuteronomy 8:1-5
Those who endure receive the crown of life.	James 1:12
People can join in one another's suffering.	2 Timothy 1:8-12
People can share in Christ's suffering.	Philippians 3:10

How to Pray with Power While Wrestling with Temptation

Throughout history, groups of Christians have separated themselves from the mainstream—even from other followers of Christ—in an attempt to avoid temptation. But their efforts have always proven to be misguided, because their objective was misguided. Can anyone avoid temptation altogether? No. That's where separatist groups get it wrong. Everyone, however, can avoid situations that are likely to prove tempting. And everyone can resist giving in to temptation by drawing on God's power. The Bible is so frank about the prevalence of temptation that the message comes through loud and clear: expect to be tempted.

✳

People may try to flee worldly enticements, but they always have with them a primary source of temptation: themselves. James 1:14-15 minces no words about that, especially in this paraphrase: "The temptation to give in to evil comes from us and only us. We have no one to blame but the leering, seducing flare-up of our own lust. Lust gets pregnant, and has a baby: sin! Sin grows up to adulthood, and becomes a real killer" (MSG).

More Than One Kind of Temptation

That's how author Eugene Peterson interpreted the words of James. But don't let that lust-related imagery fool you into thinking sexual temptation is the only kind there is.

You are tempted in the same way that everyone else is tempted. But God can be trusted not to let you be tempted too much, and he will show you how to escape from your temptations.

1 Corinthians 10:13 CEV

Since we have a great high priest who has passed through the heavens—Jesus the Son of God—let us hold fast to the confession. For we do not have a high priest who is unable to sympathize with our weaknesses, but One who has been tested in every way as we are, yet without sin.

Hebrews 4:14–15 HCSB

Think of the temptations you could face in a single day: gossiping about that new couple at church or spending money you don't have on a suit you don't need or getting back at your spouse by shutting him or her out. Those and other seemingly innocuous situations start with the urge to do something you know you shouldn't.

God Always Provides an Escape

Can you see how prevalent temptation is? Try shutting yourself off from all outside influences for just a few hours—and notice how many temptations surface during that time. But there's good news. God always provides an escape (1 Corinthians 10:13). Friends can steer you away from the temptation, or a Bible verse can give you the strength to resist. As you wrestle with temptation, show God that you are willing to take his way out—and trust him to reveal that escape route to you.

Final Thoughts

Here are five steps to help you resist temptation:

1. Acknowledge the temptation to God, yourself, and a confidant.

2. Run from the situation. If you're tempted to overeat, leave the kitchen.

3. Call to mind appropriate Bible passages (such as the "armor of God" verses in Ephesians 6:10-18).

4. Praise God. Turning toward God diverts your attention from harmful things that entice you.

5. Thank God immediately for helping you overcome the temptation.

How to Pray with Peace After Losing a Job

Mental health professionals consider the loss of a job to be a major life crisis on a par with the death of a loved one. Why? Because the stages of grief that accompany a job loss are identical to those that accompany the death of a close relative or friend: denial, anger, bargaining, depression, and eventually, acceptance. Job loss carries with it several additional complications, such as feelings of shame, embarrassment, loss of identity, and loss of self-worth. Despite such a grim diagnosis of the problem, sudden unemployment is not a hopeless situation.

✳

Unexpected Sucker Punch

Whether you've been downsized, laid off, or fired, the sudden loss of a job leaves you reeling. Even if you heard rumblings that you might lose your job, when you actually get the word, it feels like a completely unexpected sucker punch. *This isn't happening*, you immediately think. *No. This isn't possible. This can't happen to me.*

But when it does happen, your world is turned upside down. It will take time to get it turned right side up, but the sooner you turn to God in prayer, the sooner the journey through job loss will begin to go more smoothly. That's partly because prayer is proof positive that you are still in relationship with God—even if you don't understand how he could let this happen to you.

> God is our refuge and strength, an ever-present help in trouble. Therefore we will not fear, though the earth give way and the mountains fall into the heart of the sea, though its waters roar and foam and the mountains quake with their surging.
>
> Psalm 46:1–3 NIV

> The LORD gives perfect peace to those whose faith is firm. So always trust the LORD because he is forever our mighty rock.
>
> Isaiah 26:3–4 CEV

Brand-New Opportunities

Maintaining that relationship offers the best chance you have of finding needed direction and peace to think clearly about what to do next. Losing your job may open up brand-new opportunities; trusting God enables you to calmly sort out your options and make decisions based on the wisdom he gives you.

No matter what, surviving unemployment requires tenacity, perseverance, and energy, all of which are easy to lose when your job pursuit fails to yield any real opportunities. Discouragement can quickly set in. But David, who knew a thing or two about discouragement, was able to attest to the fact that the Lord "gives His people strength; the LORD blesses His people with peace" (Psalm 29:11 HCSB).

Something to Ponder

Westerners in particular often link their identity with the work they do. When they lose that work, they run the risk of losing their identity as well. Think about how closely your sense of identity is tied to the work you do, whether you have a traditional job, own a business, or work in the home. Who are you without your work?

Final Thoughts

Here are some suggestions for surviving job loss in a healthy way:

• Find a prayer and accountability partner who will come alongside and help you through this.

• Volunteer, which may or may not lead to a job, but either way, volunteering will keep you active.

• Realize that seeking work is harder than working. Have fun in the process.

How to Pray with Hope After a Natural Disaster

Insurance companies have long called tornadoes, floods, hurricanes, earthquakes, and blizzards by the ominous moniker "Acts of God." Those people left in the reality of the aftermath grit their teeth and look to heaven. There is no one else to blame for the destruction and loss. There is also no one else to go to for comfort, hope, and promise for the future. When you're hurting and anxious, how do you find the words to pray or the strength to bow your head and heart?

✳

You did not cause the natural disaster that seemed to target your family and well-being. God did not hurl the wind and stir the waves to destroy you. That is the stuff of Greek myth, not the God of the Scriptures. God loves you and mourns with you. The Bible tells us that earth has been groaning in protest, longing for the day it will be released from bondage brought on at the fall of humankind (Romans 8:18–23). As you long for restoration, realize that you—like the earth that endured the storm— are longing for heaven.

> How long, O LORD? Will You forget me forever? How long will You hide Your face from me?
>
> Psalm 13:1 NASB
>
> I have trusted in Your lovingkindness; my heart shall rejoice in Your salvation. I will sing to the LORD, because He has dealt bountifully with me.
>
> Psalm 13:5–6 NASB

The Peace That Only God Gives

God is strong enough to hear your most violent and plaintive cries. Your words cannot diminish his character or cause him to retreat from you. King David would bombard God with complaint after complaint. There is a pattern in so many of his psalms: David exhausted himself by screaming his complaints. Then he embraced the peace that only God can give.

Pray with the same force with which the storm pounded you. Then receive God's peace. The following prayer can be your road map when you have no words:

A Prayerful Road Map

God, you set the world on its foundation. You alone determine the seasons, control the wind and the waves, and make the sun to shine. Help me know your peace, feel your protection, and understand your promises for the future. Fill me with hope for tomorrow even as I am consumed with today. Help me comfort others in their losses as you comfort me in mine. Amen.

Myth Buster

Some people believe that their sins caused a natural disaster. That is simply not true. Neither does your righteousness cause the sun to shine and the birds to fly. Jesus encouraged believers to love their enemies and pray for them because God "makes His sun rise on the evil and on the good, and sends rain on the just and on the unjust" (Matthew 5:45 NKJV). Theologians call this concept *common grace*.

Final Thoughts

Phil and Christine huddled in a closet with their three young daughters as a tornado rocked their home. They emerged unharmed, but flying glass and debris had shredded their home and belongings. During the first days, cameras recorded the damage to their home, friends brought meals, and the insurance company signed a  check. Two years later, Phil and Christine finished the restoration. Long after the world moves into the next news-worthy disaster, you will still be recovering from yours. Don't lose heart.

How to Pray with Insight
About Time Management

Sometimes, it's downright baffling. The people who seem to have the fullest lives also seem to have the most time for activities like volunteering, socializing, and even taking a course or two for personal enrichment. How can that be? You imagine all sorts of things about their lives behind the scenes: they must have full-time assistants, housekeeping services, personal chefs, and live-in nannies, at the very least. Then you discover they don't have a staff attending to their everyday needs. So what gives? What's their secret? It turns out that what they have is no secret at all.

✴

Mention time-management techniques to some people, and their eyes glaze over. They feel they've heard it all before, and they don't believe any technique will work for them. You've probably heard it all as well: Write everything down. Prioritize. Limit commitments. Reduce large projects to manageable chunks. Avoid time-wasters like TV and long phone calls. Set deadlines. Just say no.

Gaining Control of Time

Those and other practical time-management suggestions are important. But gaining control of your time is as much a spiritual activity as it is a practical one. It's a matter of the heart as well as the mind. "We have time and prayer backward," wrote Christian author and philosophy professor Peter Kreeft. "We

> Come now, you who say, "Today or tomorrow we will travel to such and such a city and spend a year there and do business and make a profit." You don't even know what tomorrow will bring— what your life will be!
>
> James 4:13–14 HCSB
>
> There is an occasion for everything, and a time for every activity under heaven: a time to give birth and a time to die; a time to plant and a time to uproot.
>
> Ecclesiastes 3:1–2 HCSB

think our lack of time is the cause of our lack of prayer, but our lack of prayer is the cause of our lack of time."

Giving God Your Time

When he gives God his time, Kreeft said, he miraculously seems to have more of it: "I have no idea *how* he does it; I know *that* he does it, time after time." He compared this phenomenon to the miracle of the loaves and fishes, when Jesus took a meager offering of food, blessed it, and fed more than five thousand people with it (Matthew 14:15–21). Kreeft believes Jesus multiplies his time in much the same way.

You don't need a staff of assistants to manage your time; you need the assistance of the one who created time. Give God your time in prayer, and watch how he increases it.

Something to Ponder

Is your life all work and no pray? Consider Martin Luther's daily routine. While Luther was busy reforming the church, translating the Greek Bible into German, and dodging assaults by church leaders, he also spent time in prayer: "I generally pray two hours every day, except on very busy days. On those days, I pray three," he wrote. The more he prayed, the more productive those busy days were.

Digging Deeper

Delegating responsibility as a time-management technique is found in the Bible. When Jethro saw how much time Moses was spending settling disputes, he advised his son-in-law to appoint judges to assist him (Exodus 18). Jesus gave the twelve disciples the authority to minister in his place (Mark 6). In Acts 6, the apostles appointed others to serve the needs of the Christians in Jerusalem so they could spend more time in prayer and preaching.

How to Pray with Endurance While Raising Children

Imagine being notified that you will be required to run a marathon, a feat for which you have had no training. Actually, you would be required to run more than a marathon, much more—and its length would be measured in decades, not mere miles. There is one primary rule: no fair dropping out. That's what parenting is like, isn't it? Sure, you can try to train—caring for other people's children, reading everything in sight about parenting, absorbing the wise counsel of experienced parents. But all that pales in comparison to having your own children. For this leg of life's journey, you need endurance.

⁎

Parenting—The Hardest Work

If you ask people from all walks of life what is the hardest work they have ever done, the men and women in the group who have reared children will answer without hesitation: parenting. That's partly because it's a 24/7 job. Your children are never far from your thoughts, even when you're not physically with them, and there is tremendous responsibility involved.

There's much work to do in caring for children, many needs to anticipate, many dangers to be concerned about. And all of this is on many levels—physical, mental, emotional, and spiritual. And then there's your spouse, your friends,

> Since we are surrounded by such a huge crowd of witnesses to the life of faith, let us strip off every weight that slows us down, especially the sin that so easily trips us up. And let us run with endurance the race God has set before us.
>
> Hebrews 12:1 NLT
>
> Patient endurance is what you need now, so that you will continue to do God's will. Then you will receive all that he has promised.
>
> Hebrews 10:36 NLT

your coworkers or your staff, and your extended family, all of whom need you to some degree. Whew! Parenting is much more challenging than a simple marathon.

Learn to Pace Yourself

How will you ever make it? You need to do what every long-distance runner learns early on: you need to pace yourself.

Even for experienced runners, that's tough to do in the beginning. Runners see their competition getting way out in front; as a brand-new parent, you see a helpless infant with a seemingly endless string of needs. Slow down? No way! Cut yourself some slack. This phase will feel more like a sprint, and that's to be expected. You're doing everything for the first time.

But as your firstborn outgrows the need for your constant attention, and as more children come along, the long haul begins. This is when you need to start pacing yourself so you can run the parenting race with endurance.

Take a Break and Breathe

First, take a break and breathe—prayerfully. Praise God for the joy your children have brought into your life. Thank him for the work he is doing in the lives of your children and for bringing you through this initial stage of parenting.

Then remind yourself that this is not a competitive race. There's no point in competing to come in first. There's no point in competing against other parents. And there's no point in anticipating the finish line, because there isn't one. You will always be a parent.

Even though the culture may tell you—sometimes jokingly, sometimes not—your parenting duties are over when your child turns eighteen, you will continue to be on call as a parent for the rest of your life. Your active parenting days will subside, unless you have a special-needs child, but as a loving parent, you will always be available to your adult children.

Pray with Endurance

That means you not only have to pray for endurance, you also have to pray with endurance; you have to pray for the stamina to continue praying! It means praying during the good times as well as the bad, during the so-so times as well as the exciting times, and on the days when you don't feel like praying, when you don't feel as if God is listening, when you're not sure that your prayers are doing any good at all.

> Parents, don't be hard on your children. Raise them properly. Teach them and instruct them about the Lord.
>
> Ephesians 6:4 CEV

Keep this in mind: even when you're praying for your own endurance—the strength to continue, the energy to keep going—in a sense you're also praying for your children. A parent who feels like giving up is a testy, edgy, cranky parent who is likely to take his fatigue out on his children.

Pray that you will be the best parent you can possibly be—but only in God's power. If you try to do this on your own, everyone will suffer. Focus on the joy and on the specialness of every day. Give your children whatever you can, whenever you can, and however you can, but pace yourself in the process. They will need you all along the journey; make sure you'll be there for them.

Points to Remember

- You're in this for the long haul; pace yourself.

- This is not a competition, nor is there a finish line.

- Focus on the joy your children have brought to your life.

- Don't try to be a good parent in your own power; rely on God to give you strength.

- Pray with endurance as well as for endurance.

- Give your fatigue to God so you don't take it out on your children.

Check Your Understanding

■ **Why is parenting so difficult and so overwhelming—even when you tried to prepare for it?**

Parenting is a job that never stops; you're either meeting your children's immediate needs or anticipating the next round. There are some situations involved in parenting that you can't prepare for.

■ **Does it ever get easier?**

Yes—as long as you pace yourself. You may feel as if you're running a fifty-yard dash when your first child is born, but then you settle down into an endurance race.

■ **Won't it get even easier when they're adults?**

The everydayness of parenting will be over, but they will still need you. Your love and concern for them won't diminish. And you never know—they may end up moving back home, bringing with them an entirely different set of challenges!

Final Thoughts

Every family dynamic is different. Parenting techniques that work for one family may not work for yours. But there is one sure thing when it comes to being a parent—the wisdom you can glean from the Bible. Keep it close by and read it daily. In addition to its direct advice to parents, it has a great deal to say about relationships in general.

How to Pray in Grief While Facing Infertility

Only those who are also infertile can fully understand the pain and heartbreak of a couple unable to conceive. The desire for a child is unlike any other. You want a child that your love has produced, a girl or boy who carries not just your DNA but so much more—the essence of who you are as a couple, two people united as one. Although nearly 20 percent of all couples experience infertility at least temporarily, some infertile couples suffer from an acute, indescribable loneliness. Their yearning for a child consumes their lives.

☧

If the desire for children is consuming your life, you've probably had well-meaning friends, relatives, and acquaintances offer advice on how to improve your chances of conceiving. But none of that advice helps you endure the emotional roller coaster you experience month after month.

Pray to Strengthen Faith

Infertile Christian couples across the country have a different kind of advice for you—suggestions about how to pray to strengthen your faith in God and your relationship as a couple, as well as how to maintain your sanity. Here are some ways of praying that have helped other childless couples:

The LORD is close to the brokenhearted; he rescues those whose spirits are crushed.

Psalm 34:18 NLT

The LORD's kindness never fails! If he had not been merciful, we would have been destroyed. The LORD can always be trusted to show mercy each morning. Deep in my heart I say, "The LORD is all I need; I can depend on him!" The LORD is kind to everyone who trusts and obeys him. It is good to wait patiently for the LORD to save us.

Lamentations 3:22–26 CEV

• Be honest with God about your anger, disappointment, and doubts.

- Ask for contentment with your family of two.

- Thank God for his blessings on your life.

- Ask for compassion for struggling parents and joy for new parents.

- Seek God's purpose for your life and ways to serve him and others.

Will praying in this way erase the pain? Perhaps not, but it will likely ease the pain. And one day, despite the pain, you'll be able to utter these words with complete conviction: "Though the fig tree should not blossom and there be no fruit on the vines, though the yield of the olive should fail and the fields produce no food, though the flock should be cut off from the fold and there be no cattle in the stalls, yet I will exult in the Lord, I will rejoice in the God of my salvation" (Habakkuk 3:17–18 NASB).

Insight into Your Situation

Most of the women in the Bible who had trouble conceiving eventually gave birth. That can make you either hopeful or discouraged, depending on your perspective. But reading about their experiences—the level of their trust in God, the way they handled their infertility—may give you insight into your own situation.

Infertility in the Bible

Woman	Scripture
Elizabeth	Luke 1
Hannah	1 Samuel 1
Manoah's wife	Judges 13
Michal	2 Samuel 6
Rachel	Genesis 30
Rebekah	Genesis 25
Sarah	Genesis 16
Shunammite woman	2 Kings 4

How to Pray with Confidence Concerning Military Service

In times of economic downturn, one segment of society sees a dramatic upturn of interest in its work: the military. And why not? Military service offers a steady paycheck, great training, and enviable benefits. When little other work is available, the advantages of joining the military outweigh the dangers. But military service is much more than a smart career choice. The decision to serve your country in the armed forces is not one to be taken lightly. It requires a sense of mission and patriotism, a thorough understanding of what you may be ordered to do, and clear direction from God.

✳

Since 1973, the United States has had an all-volunteer military. Before that, young men were required to serve unless they had a legitimate reason not to. Today, young men and women alike can choose to serve, with many seeing the military as a viable option to college—or unemployment.

Pray About Your Decision to Serve

But a military career is service to your country rather than just another job. It's important to pray about your decision to serve. Military service may place you in dangerous situations where military leadership is recognized as the final authority.

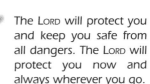

The LORD will protect you and keep you safe from all dangers. The LORD will protect you now and always wherever you go.

Psalm 121:7–8 CEV

You are my hiding place; You protect me from trouble. You surround me with joyful shouts of deliverance.

Psalm 32:7 HCSB

That's a necessary component of military life. A commanding officer must have unquestioned authority. Without it, the unit would be disorganized and be ill prepared to act. In the service, you will face difficult situations requiring your automatic and complete obedience.

How should you pray? First, be sure this is God's will for your life and not a default decision. Military service can be an honorable, rewarding career, but it's also a mission. Is the military's mission compatible with God's mission, that of defending the powerless from their enemies? If you answer yes but have misgivings, make your concerns known at the outset. Every branch of the armed forces offers opportunities to serve in ways that honor your religious beliefs. Then begin your service with enthusiasm and energy, giving it your all.

Bible Passages That Offer Assurance

You can't read very far in the Bible without coming across passages that offer assurance that God will provide safety and security and save his people from their enemies. Below are some verses that will help you believe in his care for you during your time of military service.

Psalms to Sustain You

Scripture	Words of Comfort
Psalm 4:8	I will lie down and sleep in peace, for you alone, O Lord, make me dwell in safety. (NIV)
Psalm 31:15	My life is in your hands. Save me from enemies who hunt me down. (CEV)
Psalm 32:7	You are my hiding place; You protect me from trouble. You surround me with joyful shouts of deliverance. (HCSB)
Psalm 32:8	I will guide you along the best pathway for your life. I will advise you and watch over you. (NLT)
Psalm 33:20	We wait for the Lord; He is our help and shield. (HCSB)
Psalm 41:2	You protect them and keep them alive. You make them happy here in this land, and you don't hand them over to their enemies. (CEV)
Psalm 42:5	Why are you in despair, O my soul? And why have you become disturbed within me? Hope in God, for I shall again praise Him for the help of His presence. (NASB)
Psalm 46:1	God is our refuge and strength, a very present help in trouble. (NASB)

How to Pray with Focus When Starting a New Job

So—you've landed a new job. How exciting! A fresh start, a different environment, all new coworkers . . . everything strange and unfamiliar. Maybe it's not so exciting after all. A new opportunity carries with it some old fears and some nagging questions. How steep is the learning curve? Are you up to the challenge? Will your future colleagues like you? Will you fit in? Those answers will come in time. Right now, your job is to focus on the most important question: what does God want you to accomplish in your new position?

Be Confident in Your Purpose

You may never know why God has placed you in this new job. But if you are confident God provided the job, you can also be confident that there's a purpose for your being there. That's a good place to start—asking God to accomplish his will through you at your new place of employment.

But you still have many practical concerns and questions. It's normal to feel apprehensive before your first day in a new job. The more detailed your prayers, the less anxious you're likely to feel when that day comes.

Here are some ideas to get you started:

> Pay careful attention to your own work, for then you will get the satisfaction of a job well done, and you won't need to compare yourself to anyone else.
>
> Galatians 6:4 NLT
>
> Whatever you do, do your work heartily, as for the Lord rather than for men.
>
> Colossians 3:23 NASB

- Thank God for the opportunity.
- Pray God's blessing on your new colleagues.

- Trust God to give you wisdom regarding every aspect of your job.

- Ask God for patience as you seek to understand the company before suggesting changes.

- Call upon God to help you be the best employee (or boss) you can possibly be.

- Pray that God will give you a true servant's heart and attitude in the workplace.

- Give God your fears, worries, and misgivings about your ability to perform the work that's ahead of you.

Pray in Detail

Pray in detail about your specific job; if you are a health-care professional, for example, ask God for compassion for the patients you'll be treating.

Finally, don't forget about the joy, the excitement, and the positive challenges you'll experience. Thank God in advance for all the good things to come—including that first paycheck.

Points to Remember

- God has a purpose in placing you in this new position.

- Your many questions about your new workplace will be answered in time; let go of them for now.

- Feeling nervous about starting a new job is normal.

- Praying about specific concerns will help alleviate your apprehension.

- It's okay to enjoy this new experience; allow yourself to feel joyful and excited!

How to Pray with Expectation When Getting Married

Engaged couples who are head over heels in love may read all the right books on marriage, go for extensive premarital counseling, and listen to lots of advice from those who are—or have been—married, but seldom does all that prepare them for the reality of married life. One reason is that marriage has to be experienced and not just talked about. Another reason is this: those head-over-heels-in-love couples secretly believe that they're different. No one can possibly understand their love; others just don't get it. But their marriage will set a new standard for marital bliss and success.

✴

If your expectation is for yours to be a groundbreaking marriage, that would be a great concept to start praying about. You probably also have a different and larger set of expectations. It's time to start talking to God about those as well.

A World of Two or Three

Couples often believe that all they need is each other, and that's understandable. When you first fall in love, the universe shrinks down to a world of two—or three, if you are both Christians and include God in your world. Ask God to show you how you can keep your marriage free of an unhealthy dependence on each other as your friends and coworkers gradually resume their importance in your lives.

Wives, understand and support your husbands in ways that show your support for Christ.

Ephesians 5:22 MSG

Husbands, go all out in your love for your wives, exactly as Christ did for the church—a love marked by giving, not getting.

Ephesians 5:25 MSG

Since money can cause the biggest problems in a marriage, ask God to help you and your future spouse work out some ground rules now. If one of you is a saver and the other a spender, you need to come to a consensus about your financial expectations before the wedding.

Be Prepared to Fight for Your Spouse's Faith

Right now, your future partner may have a seemingly unshakable faith in God, and you can't imagine your spouse walking away from God. But it happens. Begin praying that both of you will cling to God throughout your marriage, ramp up that prayer at the first hint of a problem, and be prepared to fight for your spouse's faith with everything you have.

List all your other expectations for your marriage, and pray about each one—now, before the wedding takes place.

Something to Ponder

Ephesians 5 contains several verses telling wives and husbands how they should relate to each other. Take a look at the married couples in your sphere of close relationships. Would their marriages be different if they took these verses to heart? Then apply the same standard to your own upcoming marriage. How can you apply the appropriate verse to your role in the relationship?

Final Thoughts

One of the greatest evidences of genuine love is wanting the best for the other person. Sometimes, what is best for your spouse will be at odds with your desires, expectations, and with what you think is best for you. That's when you'll come to an understanding of just how difficult sacrificial love can be. Make the sacrifice out of a  loving commitment to your mate, and see what God has in store for you.

How to Pray with Excitement When Graduating

As you approach graduation, you've likely been inundated with motivational messages that can be summed up in one word: possibilities. The possibilities that lie before you are endless. You can be anything you want to be. There's no limit to all you can accomplish as you begin this next stage of your life's journey. It all sounds so exciting—and so frightening. Stepping out into a world of new responsibilities and challenges can instill as much fear as enthusiasm. What many motivational messages omit, however, is the one word that can dispel that fear—*Jesus*.

"Go Out and Train Everyone"

After the resurrection, the disciples came together in the presence of their resurrected Lord. Some worshipped him without hesitation, but others held back. That didn't faze Jesus: "Jesus, undeterred, went right ahead and gave his charge: 'God authorized and commanded me to commission you: Go out and train everyone you meet, far and near, in this way of life, marking them by baptism in the threefold name: Father, Son, and Holy Spirit. Then instruct them in the practice of all I have commanded you. I'll be with you as you do this, day after day after day, right up to the end of the age'" (Matthew 28:18–20 MSG).

This is known as the commissioning of the disciples. Jesus sent them out in his power to do God's will.

> Be strong and courageous. Do not be terrified; do not be discouraged, for the LORD your God will be with you wherever you go.
>
> Joshua 1:9 NIV
>
> Don't let anyone think less of you because you are young. Be an example to all believers in what you say, in the way you live, in your love, your faith, and your purity.
>
> 1 Timothy 4:12 NLT

While their mission may have differed from yours, the final words of that passage apply to your "commission" upon graduating: Jesus will be with you as you enter this new world, every day for the rest of your life.

Charge to Transform Lives

Notice this as well. Jesus did not commission the disciples to go out and be all that they could be. His charge to you isn't about how you can succeed; rather, it is about how you can help transform lives. The world's motivational message is all about you. Jesus' words are all about serving others.

No matter what field you enter after graduation, you will be in a position to change the lives of others. What could be more exciting than that?

Myth Buster

You can be anything you want to be." Those are high-sounding words that many a commencement speaker has uttered. But they simply aren't true. God gives each person certain talents and strengths, and when people use their gifts to their fullest, everyone benefits. You can be any number of things, but you will be most fulfilled when you do whatever it is that God created you to do. And that's no myth.

Something to Ponder

Do you want success? Meditate on this: "God blesses those people who refuse evil advice and won't follow sinners or join in sneering at God. Instead, the Law of the LORD makes them happy, and they think about it day and night. They are like trees growing beside a stream, trees that produce fruit in season and always have leaves. Those people succeed in everything they do" (Psalm 1:1–3 CEV).

How to Pray in Sympathy When Someone Has Died

At some point in your life, you may have been on the receiving end of condolences when a loved one died. What do you remember about the expressions of sympathy you received? Most likely, the ones you recall fall into one of two categories: unbelievably insensitive or incredibly helpful. What does that tell you about the best way to show your sympathy when a friend or acquaintance is grieving? For one thing, it tells you that being incredibly helpful has a lasting positive effect on the one in mourning.

✢

Many people are at a loss when it comes to expressing their condolences when someone they know has lost a loved one. They're so afraid of saying the wrong thing that they end up doing just that. "I know just how you feel," a neighbor may say to a woman who just lost her mother. "My cat died last month." That kind of comment is memorable, but only for being entirely inappropriate.

For Christians, the standard sympathetic comment is this: "I'll be praying for you." There's nothing wrong with that on the surface; mourners often appreciate knowing others are praying for them, and it helps smooth over the awkwardness of the situation.

> Rejoice with those who rejoice, and weep with those who weep.
>
> Romans 12:15 NKJV
>
> Bear one another's burdens, and so fulfill the law of Christ.
>
> Galatians 6:2 NKJV

But what if you want to go deeper than the surface? What would your prayer sound like then?

Add God–Acts to God–Talk

Here is a good place to start. For a different kind of prayer, look to the book of James: "Dear friends, do you think you'll get anywhere in this if you learn all the right words but never do anything? Does merely talking about faith indicate that a person really has it? For instance, you come upon an old friend dressed in rags and half-starved and say, 'Good morning, friend! Be clothed in Christ! Be filled with the  Holy Spirit!' and walk off without providing so much as a coat or a cup of soup—where does that get you? Isn't it obvious that God-talk without God-acts is outrageous nonsense?" (2:14–17 MSG). Place that in the context of grief, and ask God how you can add some God-acts to your God-talk.

People experiencing grief often have many practical needs, but they can be so focused on their loss that they find it impossible to articulate those needs. Telling your friend something along the lines of "Let me know how I can help" may sound like the right thing to say, but it places the burden on the mourner to think clearly and try to remember what needs to be done. But when you utter those same words to God, they become a prayer that results in God-talk in action.

Offer Practical Help Without Being Intrusive

John 11 tells of people coming from all around Jerusalem to comfort Mary and Martha when they learned of their brother's death. That way of expressing sympathy hasn't changed in two thousand years; friends, neighbors, and acquaintances want to do something, which often means bringing the grieving person a casserole to eliminate the need to cook. But it also means that mourners often find themselves overwhelmed with company. As you're praying that God will comfort your friend, pray also that God will show you how you can provide practical help without being intrusive. That could mean cleaning her house while she's at the funeral home making arrangements, but it could also mean forgetting about the house and going to the funeral home with her.

Throughout this time of mourning, continue praying in the same way. If you've lost a loved one, you know how lonely you can feel weeks and months later, when the cards and company have stopped arriving. Seek God's wisdom on how you can continue to serve and help the one who is still in mourning long after the other people in his life have become busy with their own lives. God may choose to use you to show his continued love and compassion toward your grieving friend.

> Many people had come from the city to comfort Martha and Mary because their brother had died.
>
> John 11:19 CEV

Walk Alongside Your Friend

Most of all, your friend will need someone who is willing to "come alongside" and quietly walk with her on the difficult path of mourning. Pray that God will give you that willingness, along with his wisdom and the right words of comfort at the right time, so you can be a true representative of Christ in her life.

Something to Ponder

Not everyone feels comfortable being prayed for by others. Someone who is grieving a loss will seldom be able to say no when asked if it's okay to pray with him. If you sense that the person would prefer that you not pray, remember that there's nothing wrong with simply sitting with her and praying silently. God will still hear your prayer.

Check Your Understanding

- **What's wrong with saying, "I know just how you feel"?**

Everything. Each person's grief is intensely personal, and each person's relationship with the one who died is unique. Even if your losses are similar—her mother just died, and yours died recently—you can't possibly know just how she feels.

- **What's wrong with saying, "I'll be praying for you"?**

Nothing. It is something of a default comment, though, and it's much more helpful when you customize your prayers specifically to the person's needs.

- **What's wrong with saying, "Let me know how I can help"?**

It's an open-ended offer that forces a grieving person to divert his thinking in a whole different direction. It's much better for you to do the thinking for him by asking God how you can help and then going to the person with specific, practical suggestions.

Final Thoughts

 In years past, it was a common practice for people to write a note or a letter to a person in mourning. As greeting cards became commonplace, that practice fell by the wayside. In today's culture of e-mails and instant messaging, receiving a handwritten letter is a memorable occurrence. Consider reviving that practice. Your friend will no doubt appreciate a condolence letter that recounts fond memories of the one who has died.

How to Pray When You Are Afraid

Terrorist attacks. Terminal illnesses. Plane crashes, car crashes, stock market crashes. Things that go bump in the night. And landing in the number one spot on many polls, public speaking. There seems to be no limit to things people fear. Throughout the Bible God told his people to not be afraid. How can you not be afraid when terrible things happen every day? The nightly news and personal experience confirm that. Is there some secret formula for making fear disappear?

⋇

Controlling Your Fears

Your fears may never disappear entirely, but you can learn to control them instead of allowing them to control you. God's formula for letting go of fear is no secret, though. It's written on page after page in the Bible, in passages as clear and direct as this one: "Do not fear, for I am with you; do not be dismayed, for I am your God. I will strengthen you and help you; I will uphold you with my righteous right hand. . . . For I am the LORD, your God, who takes hold of your right hand and says to you, Do not fear; I will help you" (Isaiah 41:10, 13 NIV).

Look closely at those verses. Stop and meditate on the precise language God used: God is with you. He is your God. He will make you strong. He will come to your aid, grasping your right hand and keeping you standing with his own right hand—his righteous right hand. And he will tell you, directly and in no uncertain terms, not to be afraid. He will help you.

> The LORD is my light and my salvation; whom shall I fear? The LORD is the strength of my life; of whom shall I be afraid?
>
> Psalm 27:1 NKJV

> What then? I will pray with the spirit, and I will also pray with my understanding. I will sing with the spirit, and I will also sing with my understanding.
>
> 1 Corinthians 14:15 HCSB

Weapons in Your Spiritual Arsenal

Those are more than words of comfort. Countless Christians can attest to the very real presence of God in the face of unspeakable horror as well as everyday fears. When fear threatens to overwhelm you, pull out two of the most powerful weapons in your spiritual arsenal—the Bible and prayer—and fight fear head-on. You may find yourself above it, no longer cowering under its tyranny.

Something to Ponder

How you answer these questions may help you better understand your relationship with fear: What are you really afraid of? Is this a legitimate or an irrational fear? Do you believe God will see you through this, regardless of the outcome? Have you prayed to the point of experiencing genuine peace? Why do you think God has allowed this fear-inducing situation to continue? How has your fear helped the situation?

Final Thoughts

Remember that fear can be beneficial, warning you of real dangers—but God's admonition to not be afraid still applies. Violent-crime survivors often describe feeling fear immediately before an attack, as do would-be victims who responded to fear and escaped unharmed. The key is acting on the warning rather than remaining afraid. Discerning the difference between legitimate and irrational fear requires spiritual vigilance—a continual alertness to God's direction.

How to Pray When You Are Angry

Another driver cuts you off in rush-hour traffic, a coworker sabotages your chance to get the recognition you deserve, the city increases your property tax by 20 percent, your daughter manages once again to leave the house without cleaning her room—and that's all in one day. It's enough to make anyone see red. Before you vent your anger inappropriately—giving in to road rage, undermining your colleague, calling the mayor at home at 3 a.m., grounding your firstborn for the rest of her life—stop a minute and think. Think about how God wants you to respond.

✤

The Bible frequently addresses the problem of anger. In some cases, the anger is justified, as when Jesus overturned the tables of the temple moneychangers (Matthew 21:12-13). But when the Bible addresses the problem of not-so-righteous anger, it's clear that such anger needs to be dealt with.

Not-So-Righteous Anger

The ideal method is to ask God to calm you down, resolve the problem that caused your rage, and restore relationships that were damaged in the heat of your anger. All that can come to pass, but it often doesn't. Thankfully, God has provided a way for you to release your anger when your thoughts are so clouded you can't pray as you normally would and you feel as if your fury is eating you up inside.

> Stop being angry! Turn from your rage! Do not lose your temper—it only leads to harm. For the wicked will be destroyed, but those who trust in the LORD will possess the land.
>
> Psalm 37:8–9 NLT

> My dearly loved brothers, understand this: everyone must be quick to hear, slow to speak, and slow to anger, for man's anger does not accomplish God's righteousness.
>
> James 1:19–20 HCSB

The way he has provided is found in the Psalms.

Right there, amid lovely passages about green pastures and still waters, you'll find psalms in which the writers lashed out in anger. Christians through the centuries have found value in venting their feelings by praying these "angry psalms" (Psalms 7; 13; and 55, for example) back to God. Instead of verbally attacking the people who angered them, they expressed themselves honestly to someone who already knew how they felt.

A Word of Warning

A word of warning: some of these psalms are challenging to modern sensibilities; use discernment in deciding which to pray. In most cases, the psalmist's anger eventually dissipates, and he places his trust in God—not a bad way for an angry prayer to end.

Many people have found it helpful to ward off anger by learning and practicing ways to control their emotions in advance. The following chart lists some methods for managing anger.

Some Do's and Don'ts for Controlling Anger

Do...	Don't...
Meditate on Bible verses that refer to anger. Seek out the godly counsel of others who can help you overcome the anger you're experiencing.	Retaliate by reacting to the situation in the heat of your anger.
Forgive the one who made you angry—even if it's yourself.	Say anything right away. You'll likely regret it.
Express your anger through prayer, journaling, or talking with a counselor of trusted friend. Let it out to the right person at the right time.	Seek revenge. Even if you don't retaliate right away, you may be tempted to engage in some, calculating, coldhearted revenge later on. Don't.
Practice compassion by recognizing the pain in the lives of others. Learn how to avoid defensiveness.	Hold it in. Venting your anger appropriately is healthy for body, mind, and spirit.
Choose peace. Calm your mind and your spirit; relax by giving the situation to God.	Be defensive. Defensiveness— deflecting criticism by trying to justify your behavior—empowers others, not you.

How to Pray When You Are Depressed

Depression is a serious, paralyzing disorder so complex that the medical community continues to learn more about it, thousands of years after it was first described in ancient writings. But one thing they learned long ago is this: no one is immune to depression, and that includes Christians. If you are suffering from depression, you know how crippling it is. You're vaguely aware that help is available, but you can't take the first step toward getting help. God seems so far away that you doubt he could hear your prayers, if you could even find the will to pray them.

✳

Frustrating Aspects of Depression

One of the most frustrating aspects of depression is the fact that the steps depressives can take to get better are the very things they find impossible: changing their thought patterns, seeking medical attention, enlisting the support of family and friends, establishing healthy routines—and praying. Medical professionals recognize the power of prayer to help overcome the debilitating effects of depression, even if the depressed patient isn't the one praying; the prayers of the patient's circle of relationships can have a profound effect on her recovery.

Still, for any treatment to be fully effective, the depressed person—you—must be actively involved. So how do you take that first step? Take a cue from some prominent figures in Israel's history—David, Elijah, and Jeremiah, among others.

> I am convinced that neither death, nor life, nor angels, nor principalities, nor things present, nor things to come, nor powers, nor height, nor depth, nor any other created thing, will be able to separate us from the love of God, which is in Christ Jesus our Lord.
>
> Romans 8:38–39 NASB

> The LORD is my rock, my fortress and my deliverer; my God is my rock, in whom I take refuge.
>
> Psalm 18:2 NIV

All three suffered from depression, but their means of dealing with it may be a lesson to twenty-first-century believers. They didn't deny it; they acknowledged it and at times lashed out at God in the midst of their pain. That may not seem very nice, but their railing at God was an honest expression of prayer.

Tell God About Your Suffering

Are you suffering? Tell God all about it. He already knows, but he's waiting to hear from you; he wants a restored relationship with you so your healing can begin. Venting your anger, your pain, your hopelessness, your despair may not seem like praying, but it may be one of the most important prayers you will ever utter.

Something to Ponder

Author Sheila Walsh once said of her period of severe depression, "I never knew God lived so close to the floor." Lying on the floor in a mental-health facility and discovering that God was right there with her helped reverse the downward progression of the disorder for her. Wherever depression has led you—isolated, unable to leave the house, unable to relate to anyone—imagine that God is right there with you, because he is.

Myth Buster

You may think that no one at church will understand. Christians are half as likely to become depressed as the general population, but that means it is likely that some in your own faith community have had firsthand experience with depression and will understand. Some Christians believe that taking antidepressants shows a lack of faith. Taking medication, however, shows you have faith that God has revealed to medical researchers the ideal chemical balance the brain needs to function properly.

How to Pray When You Doubt God

Doubt is a vexing problem for many Christians. They wonder how they can be true Christians if they have doubts, and so they resist seeking the counsel of more mature Christians. They wonder what their pastors would think of them. And they wonder if their friends would brand them as "nonbelievers." From Abraham and Peter to Billy Graham and Mother Teresa, stalwarts of the faith have expressed doubt. Some, like Abraham, had their doubts erased after witnessing a genuine miracle. Others found their faith restored by tenaciously pursuing the answers to their questions. They discovered that doubt strengthened their faith.

An Astonishing Secret

Ten years after Mother Teresa's 1997 death, the world learned an astonishing secret about her. This loving, compassionate nun who had devoted her life to the poorest of the poor experienced such intense spiritual pain that she doubted the existence of God and heaven throughout the latter years of her ministry. So shocking was this revelation that it made headlines around the world; major news services, networks, and newsmagazines gave the story prominent play, a rarity for news about a religious figure.

> Jesus said . . . , "If you can believe, all things are possible to him who believes." Immediately the father of the child cried out and said with tears, "Lord, I believe; help my unbelief!"
>
> Mark 9:23–24 NKJV
>
> Let him ask in faith without doubting. For the doubter is like the surging sea, driven and tossed by the wind.
>
> James 1:6 HCSB

Meanwhile, many Christians around the world breathed a nearly audible sigh of relief. After years or decades of harboring their own doubts about God, they learned they were neither inferior nor alone. In her private correspondence, Mother Teresa, one of the most admired personalities of the twentieth century, admitted to experiencing a great "silence and emptiness"; her letters exposed the interior life of a believer in crisis who confessed that spiritual dryness, darkness, loneliness, and torture characterized her days.

The Nature of Religious Doubt

In the wake of these revelations, prominent Christian leaders weighed in on the nature of religious doubt. What emerged from this public discussion about a controversial theological concept provided even greater relief for doubting Christians everywhere. Perhaps for the first time, they

heard theologians make the crucial distinction between doubt and disbelief, affirm the importance of doubt as an integral part of the faith journey, and describe doubt as the fertilizer that enables faith to grow.

What does all this mean for you? Doubting God means you are thinking about him—who he is, if he is, what he's like, why he doesn't do what you expect him to. This exploration proves you haven't dismissed him as nonexistent or irrelevant; he is important to you, even if you're not so sure about everything you've been taught to believe about him. Where there is doubt, there is also hope.

Questions as a Springboard to Faith

With that in mind, you can begin to look at your questions about God as a springboard to faith. Even in her darkest days, Mother Teresa never stopped serving or praying to the God she wasn't so sure of. Despite your doubts, continue to do the same. Talk to God about every one of your concerns even if it feels as if you're talking to the walls that surround you. Be honest and open and real with God. If this is the genuine cry of your heart, begin with the words from the gospel of Mark that have given many Christians a prayer to pray when no other words would come: "Lord, I believe; help my unbelief!" (9:24 NKJV).

As you continue to hold out hope that your faith will be restored and you'll find at least some of the answers you're seeking, enlist the support of trustworthy believers. They will encourage you to examine the biblical evidence of who God is, and they will pray for you as you walk this path of uncertainty. You may be surprised to discover that many people who are so strong in their faith today got to that point after a long and intense struggle over what they truly believed.

> [Jesus] said to Thomas, "Put your finger here; see my hands. Reach out your hand and put it into my side. Stop doubting and believe." Thomas said to him, "My Lord and my God!" Then Jesus told him, "Because you have seen me, you have believed; blessed are those who have not seen and yet have believed."
>
> John 20:27–29 NIV

You Are in Good Company

Regardless of how alone you may still feel, remember that you are in good company. Jesus himself felt as if God had abandoned him as he cried out on the cross, "My God, My God, why have You forsaken Me?" (Matthew 27:46 NKJV). Martin Luther echoed those same words after the Roman Catholic Church excommunicated him for renouncing certain doctrines. "My God, my God, do you hear me? Are you dead? Are you dead? No, you can't die. You can only hide yourself, can't you?" Luther asked, questioning the reality of God's presence.

Confess your doubt to the God you're not so sure of. He has heard it all before, and he has given some of his greatest doubters a reason to believe. Allow him to do the same for you.

Digging Deeper

If you have serious doubts about God—his existence, his love for you and humanity, his willingness and ability to make things right in a world gone wrong— spend time in deep reflection thinking about what you actually do believe. Then turn to the Gospels and read what Jesus said about faith and doubt, praying as you do that God will reveal himself to you and help you to have faith in him once again.

Check Your Understanding

■ **Does your doubt about God mean that you are no longer a Christian?**

Absolutely not. It means only that you are a Christian who has questions that need to be answered. The fact that you are concerned about the authenticity of your faith underscores your desire to find those answers and have your assurance in God restored.

■ **Is it possible to have complete certainty about everything relating to God, Jesus, and the Bible?**

Some people seem to, but this side of heaven it's unlikely. God has revealed a great deal, but he has also withheld much. Certainty leaves little room for faith. God wants you to trust him for the things you don't understand and rely on him to give you greater understanding when the time is right.

Points to Remember

• Doubt is not the same as disbelief.

• You can continue to serve God during a time of questioning.

• Doubt is the fertilizer that causes faith to grow.

• Your uncertainty about God is a healthy sign that you are thinking deeply about him.

• Your doubts will never separate you from the love of God.

• Times of doubting are a normal component of faith.

• Many well-known Christian leaders have experienced extended periods of doubt.

How to Pray When You Are Jealous

If ever there was a perfect setup for a lifetime of jealousy and ill will, it was the plan hatched by a man named Laban. After promising that Jacob could marry his beautiful daughter Rachel, Laban pulled a fast one and tricked Jacob into marrying his homely daughter Leah. When Jacob got angry with him, Laban shrugged it off but wanted to make it right—so he let Jacob marry Rachel as well. Do you see the potential for maximum jealousy here? But wait. The story actually gets worse.

✤

Jacob's love for Rachel was obvious to everyone. That made Leah jealous—until she became the favored one in the culture of the time by bearing seven children and using them to win over Jacob. Rachel would have none of that. In a jealous rage, she demanded that Jacob give her children as well.

Deadly Consequences of Jealousy

Rachel got her demand at the price of her own life. After delivering a healthy child, Joseph, she died giving birth to a second child. Jealousy can have deadly consequences, and it can be passed from one generation to another. Jacob not only preferred one wife over another, he also preferred one child over others. Of all his children, he loved Joseph the most. And Joseph's siblings hated him for it.

If you are struggling with jealousy, turn to God immediately. When jealousy is allowed to fester, it

> Let us walk with decency, as in the daylight: not in carousing and drunkenness; not in sexual impurity and promiscuity; not in quarreling and jealousy.
>
> Romans 13:13 HCSB
>
> Wherever there is jealousy and selfish ambition, there you will find disorder and evil of every kind.
>
> James 3:16 NLT

breeds bitterness, resentment, and hatred. It will hurt you far more than it will hurt the other person. Nothing good can come from a spirit of jealousy.

The Simple but Not Easy Antidote

The antidote is simple but not easy. It begins with a prayer of blessing for the person. That may seem difficult, even impossible, but ridding your life of jealousy requires bold, tough action. Ask God to give you power over your negative feelings. Ask him to open your eyes to his work in the life of the person you envy so you may begin to have compassion on him or her—and maybe even love the person.

Jealousy is nothing new. God's people have been dealing with it since the family of Adam and Eve.

Examples of Jealousy in the Bible

Persons	Scriptures
Cain and Abel	Genesis 4
Hired hands	Matthew 20
Jewish leaders and apostles	Acts 5
Jews and Paul, Silas	Acts 17
Joseph and his brothers	Genesis 37
Korah and Moses	Numbers 16; Psalm 106
Moses and Aaron, Miriam	Numbers 12
Prodigal son's brother	Luke 15
Rachel and Leah	Genesis 30
Saul and David	1 Samuel 18

How to Pray When You Feel Exhausted

Are you among the millions of Americans who hurry from one activity to another, working day and night, living lives of constant exhaustion? Maybe you are also involved in ministry; whether it's full-time or part-time, paid or voluntary, ministry can be more draining than any other activity. You're weary, run-down, and so overtired that the little sleep you get doesn't revive you. You need a break. What if someone offered you a free, fail-proof, guaranteed opportunity to take that break? You would take it, right? Well, Someone has, and you would do well to take it. It's called the Sabbath.

⁂

Understanding the Sabbath

Keeping the Sabbath begins with understanding what that means. In some Jewish and Christian traditions, it is characterized by a long list of rules governing what can and cannot be done on the day recognized as the Sabbath. If that's your context for understanding the Sabbath, it's no wonder you don't observe it; following all those rules is hard work and is not exactly a break from your routine.

Jesus never encouraged that kind of Sabbath-keeping. Instead, he considered the Sabbath to be a gift from God: "The Sabbath was made to serve us; we weren't made to serve the Sabbath," he said (Mark 2:27 MSG). The Sabbath provides us with a priceless opportunity to stop, catch our breath, and experience a day unlike any other in the week.

> Those who trust in the LORD will find new strength. They will soar high on wings like eagles. They will run and not grow weary. They will walk and not faint.
>
> Isaiah 40:31 NLT
>
> Come to me, all of you who are weary and carry heavy burdens, and I will give you rest. Take my yoke upon you. Let me teach you, because I am humble and gentle at heart, and you will find rest for your souls. For my yoke is easy to bear, and the burden I give you is light.
>
> Matthew 11:28–30 NLT

Stopping for a Full Day

How can you stop for a full day? The need never stops; how can you? Interestingly, studies have shown that people are more productive when they work six days and take an entire day off than if they spread their work over seven days. A day of rest, relaxation, and life-enriching activities makes people more creative, energized, and effective at what they do on the other six days. (If you work on Sunday, keep the Sabbath on another day.)

Thank God for the precious gift of a day of rest. Ask him how you can rearrange your life to take advantage of the Sabbath—and how to rearrange the other six days to take advantage of the life he has given you.

Points to Remember

- Reducing your responsibilities is not an indication of weakness; it's a sign of wisdom.

- If you think your work is indispensable, you are taking your work too seriously.

- Fatigue is not a fruit of the Spirit (Galatians 5:22-23).

- Taking a walk and breathing deeply are two of the best physical remedies for exhaustion—and both are free.

Something to Ponder

With few exceptions—say, a single parent working two jobs to survive—people end up exhausted because they overcommit or can't say no when others make demands on their time. Their choices may be well-intended, but the results can be harmful. Instead of wondering why you are so tired, you'll find it more beneficial to reflect on the answer to this question: why do you choose to live the way you do?

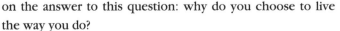

How to Pray During Illness

Everyone gets sick from time to time. Illness is never pleasant, but temporary illness is generally tolerable. You rest for a while, maybe take some medication, pray for a speedy recovery, and eventually you're back on your feet again. But chronic illness? That's another matter entirely, one that requires an often extraordinary amount of medical attention, patience, faith, and support. The prayers you pray take on a dramatically different tone. You would certainly appreciate a speedy recovery, but you find yourself praying instead to simply make it through the day.

⁂

The Centers for Disease Control estimates that nearly one-third of all Americans—not just adults but children as well—suffer from some kind of chronic disorder. Despite medical advances, that proportion is expected to rise, given the often unhealthy lifestyles of Americans and the high number of people who lack health insurance and can't afford to pay for the medical care they need.

Chronic Illness

That means it's likely that you or someone close to you is suffering from chronic illness. "Chronic illness," of course, is a relative term; a person with progressive multiple sclerosis may not agree that someone with environmental allergies is "suffering." But even though the severity of chronic disorders may vary considerably, those hundred million Americans with persistent ailments share one thing in common: the everydayness of their care.

> For you who fear My name, the sun of righteousness will rise with healing in its wings; and you will go forth and skip about like calves from the stall.
>
> Malachi 4:2 NASB
>
> Don't consider yourself to be wise; fear the LORD and turn away from evil. This will be healing for your body and strengthening for your bones.
>
> Proverbs 3:7–8 HCSB

Whether you are a diabetic facing insulin injections, a cancer patient on chemo treatments, or a victim of celiac disease for whom a grain of wheat could have debilitating consequences, the attention your illness requires begins to rule your life, and the illness itself comes to define who you are.

Bigger Than Illness

But you are much bigger than your illness, and the primary definition of who you are lies in these words: *child of God*. Every aspect of your life is important to God. So while he cares about the pain, discomfort, progression, and even cost of your illness, he sees the bigger picture of who you are. Understanding this is critical to deciding how you should pray about your present condition.

There is no question that praying for healing is appropriate. Healing was central to Jesus' earthly ministry, and the Bible encourages praying for healing and having faith that you will be healed. Praying only for healing, however, places your focus on your illness.

By contrast, praying for the presence of God as you endure this ordeal places the focus on God and your relationship with him—a focus that transcends your physical condition and encompasses all that you are.

Healing-Centered Prayer

In fact, healing-centered prayer is a fairly recent development in church history. Previous generations of believers accepted illness as a part of life and prayed that their suffering would draw them closer to God, deliver them from a complaining spirit, and instill in them the virtue of patience, among other outcomes. Today, people joke that praying for patience carries with it the danger that God will place you in some terrible, patience-trying circumstance, but in earlier times Christians considered patience a virtue critical to their moral development and ability to please God. The need to pray for that virtue simply came with whatever disorder they suffered from.

Here are some other ways you can pray in the face of serious illness:

- Tell God your fears This is not a time to pretend that all is well. Besides, God knows that isn't the truth.

- Ask God for the strength to endure the everyday complications your illness creates as well as the major events like surgery or dialysis treatments.

- Pray for God to surround you with a team of friends, family, believers, and pastoral and health-care professionals who will come alongside you and help you through this trial.

- Call upon the Holy Spirit to become the comforter you need; ask him to give you the peace, the power, and the grace to make it through each day and each night.

A More Intimate Relationship with God

Don't allow the everydayness of your chronic condition to define who you are. Instead, allow the everydayness of your prayer life to bring you into a more intimate relationship with God, the one who made you in his own whole, complete, and perfect image.

Carry that image with you throughout each day. In God's sight, you are the healthy person he made you to be.

> Your healing shall spring forth speedily, and your righteousness shall go before you.
>
> Isaiah 58:8 NKJV

References to healing appear throughout the Bible. Examples of healing in the New Testament show the many facets of the healing ministries of Jesus and the apostles.

Selected New Testament Passages on Illness and Healing

Scripture	Illness and Healing
Matthew 4:23-24	Jesus' ministry of healing.
Matthew 8:2-4	Jesus heals a leper.
Matthew 8:5-13	The centurion's son.
Matthew 8:14-15	Peter's mother.
Matthew 8:16	Healing of the demon-possessed.
Matthew 9:32-33	Healing of a mute man.
Matthew 10:1	Healing authority of the disciples.
Matthew 12:9-13	Restoration of a withered hand.
Matthew 12:22	Healing of a blind and mute man.
Matthew 15:30-31	Jesus heals a multitude of diseases and disorders.
Matthew 17:14-18	Healing of an epileptic.
Mark 16:17-18	Jesus' promise to his disciples.
Luke 4:40	Jesus heals various diseases.
Luke 6:18	People troubled by "unclean spirits" are cured.
Luke 13:10-13	Jesus heals a woman on the Sabbath.
Luke 18:35-42	Man's sight restored by his faith.
John 11:1-44	Jesus raises Lazarus from the dead.
Acts 3:1-8	Peter heals a paralytic in the name of Jesus.
Acts 5:14-16	People come to Jerusalem from outlying areas to be healed.
Acts 9:32-35	Man paralyzed and bedridden for eight years is healed.
Acts 10:38	Jesus healed people through the anointing of the Holy Spirit.
Acts 14:8-10	Paul sees faith for healing in a man who had never walked.
Acts 19:11-12	People are healed by garments touched by Paul.
Acts 28:8	Father of Publius is healed after Paul prays for him and lays hands on him.
Romans 8:11	The Spirit gives life to mortal bodies.
1 Corinthians 12:9	Holy Spirit gives the gift of healing.
James 5:14-16	Prayer for the sick.
3 John 1:2	Prayer for health.

How to Pray When Under Financial Distress

In the summer of 2008, people in the U.S. agonized over the skyrocketing cost of gasoline. Within months, though, a much bigger problem hit—a global financial crisis the likes of which few people alive today had ever seen. Many had to face some challenging and painful questions: Where had they placed their trust? Was it in the stocks they owned? The equity in their home? A steady paycheck? A steady job? All were in jeopardy, if not already gone. Or did they genuinely trust God, as many had once claimed?

✴

Where Is Your Trust?

There's nothing like financial loss to reveal where you have placed your trust. In the wake of any economic problem, many Christians who think they have been relying on God discover they were actually counting on a certain measure of stability. As long as they had a steady income, a decent roof over their heads, and some money in the bank, it was easy to believe they were trusting God with their finances.

But when things happen that change all that—like a job loss or an emergency that depletes their emergency fund—Christians are sometimes forced to face the reality that they weren't trusting God; they were trusting God to keep things normal. They had relied on money, but as author Max Lucado put it, "Money is a fickle lover, and we just got dumped."

> My God shall supply all your need according to His riches in glory by Christ Jesus.
>
> Philippians 4:19 NKJV
>
> The Spirit of the Lord is on me, because he has anointed me to preach good news to the poor. He has sent me to proclaim freedom for the prisoners and recovery of sight for the blind, to release the oppressed, to proclaim the year of the Lord's favor.
>
> Luke 4:18–19 NIV

It's Never Too Late to Trust God

The good news is that it's never too late to start trusting God. But what will you trust him for? Will you trust him only for a windfall? Nothing is impossible with God, but the greater likelihood is that he wants his people to learn a thing or two through any crisis. Pray instead that God will reveal to you his greater purpose in whatever type of financial distress you are experiencing.

Most of all, remember God's infinite love for you. Your finances are important to God, and he wants you to trust him to provide (Philippians 4:19). And remember this: God is not a fickle lover, and he will never dump you.

Nearly half of the parables Jesus told relate in some way to money.

Parables About Money

Parable	Scripture
Fishing net	Matthew 13:47–48
Good Samaritan	Luke 10:30–37
Hidden treasure	Matthew 13:44
Importuned friend	Luke 11:5–13
Laborers in the vineyard	Matthew 20:1–16
Lost piece of silver	Luke 15:8–10
Pearl of great price	Matthew 13:45–46
Pharisee and tax collector	Luke 18:9–14
Prodigal son	Luke 15:11–32
Rich fool	Luke 12:16–21
Talents	Matthew 25:14–30
Ten coins	Luke 19:12–27
Ten virgins	Matthew 25:1–13
Two debtors	Luke 7:41–43
Two sons	Matthew 21:28–32
Unjust steward	Luke 16:1–13
Unmerciful servant	Matthew 18:23–35

How to Pray in the Midst of Family Strife

Every family has problems—every family. But when your own family is in crisis, it's tempting to look at other families and convince yourself that they have it all together. The parents are as much in love today as they were on their wedding day, the children obediently clean their rooms and do their homework and never talk back, and there's never any interference from extended family members. Don't kid yourself. You don't know what goes on behind closed doors. But that doesn't matter. What matters is what's going on behind the closed doors of your own home.

※

Coping with Problems

Is your family in trouble right now? The nature of that trouble can take many forms. Every family has its own dynamic, with its members relating to one another in ways that are unique to that family. That can create a special bond, but it can also present challenges when it comes to coping with family problems or resolving them.

Equally challenging is praying for your family when turmoil seems to rule every day and when you're the one bearing the brunt of the strife, perhaps even the most direct victim of it. You may not feel like praying, particularly for those who stirred up the strife. You may feel as if there's no point; your spouse already left, your children blame you for the split, and it's too late to make a difference.

Always be humble and gentle. Be patient with each other, making allowance for each other's faults because of your love.

Ephesians 4:2 NLT

Don't use foul or abusive language. Let everything you say be good and helpful, so that your words will be an encouragement to those who hear them.

Ephesians 4:29 NLT

Never Too Late to Pray

It's never too late to pray, but it's not always easy. Regardless of the current conflict, God has placed each person where he or she is for a reason. Go to God in prayer and thank him for each and every one—no matter how difficult or disobedient or unfaithful he or she may have been—and seek God's wisdom for the situation. Pray that peace will descend on your household so you may resolve the conflict together, as a family. Most of all, pray that God will reveal himself and his love to every member of your family. Trust him to settle the conflict—and keep on praying.

Digging Deeper

Abigail was a woman of good reputation who was married to an evil and amazingly foolish man named Nabal. When Nabal brusquely dismissed David's men, refusing their request for food and drink, David and four hundred of his soldiers sought revenge. Abigail learned what had happened, but instead of blaming and dishonoring her husband, she acted wisely to prevent bloodshed. You can read how she defused this potentially disastrous situation in 1 Samuel 25.

Points to Remember

• There are no perfect, problem-free families.

• The focus needs to be kept on your own family.

• It's never too late to pray about a family problem.

• God loves each member of your family, regardless of what anyone has done to cause trouble.

• God wants each member of your family to be in relationship with him.

• Peaceful resolution is one goal, but the greater goal is seeing God's purpose come to pass.

How to Pray When You Are Worried

Are you a worrier? Lots of people are, including Christians who believe they have placed their faith and trust in God. Worry has become so tightly woven into the fabric of their lives that they don't recognize their fretting as a betrayal of the faith they profess. Think about your typical prayer time and then answer this question: when you pray, do you cast your cares on God and experience the peace of knowing it's all in his hands?

For some people, prayer has become simply worrying out loud. You hear it in their voices when they pray aloud in a group; you see it in their expressions when they utter their prayer requests. Worry lines are so deeply etched on their faces that it's evident that anxiety and dread are equally entrenched in their lives.

Time to Gain Control

Maybe you aren't a chronic worrier, but you've experienced enough apprehension about the terrible possibilities in life to know that anxiety is jeopardizing your faith relationship with God. You know it's time to gain control over the anxiety that has crept into your life.

You also know how to do that. You need to cast your cares on Jesus, because he cares for you (1 Peter 5:7). But knowing that and doing

Can all your worries add a single moment to your life? And why worry about your clothing? Look at the lilies of the field and how they grow. They don't work or make their clothing, yet Solomon in all his glory was not dressed as beautifully as they are.

Matthew 6:27–29 NLT

Don't fret or worry. Instead of worrying, pray. Let petitions and praises shape your worries into prayers, letting God know your concerns. Before you know it, a sense of God's wholeness, everything coming together for good, will come and settle you down. It's wonderful what happens when Christ displaces worry at the center of your life.

Philippians 4:6–7 MSG

Real prayer comes not from gritting our
teeth but from falling in love.

Richard Foster

Call on me when you are in trouble, and I will
rescue you, and you will give me glory.

Psalm 50:15 NLT

The LORD is near all who call out to Him,
all who call out to Him with integrity.

Psalm 145:18 HCSB

Books in The Indispensable Guide to Practically Everything
series include:

The Indispensable Guide to Practically Everything:
The Bible

The Indispensable Guide to Practically Everything:
Bible Prophecy and the End Times

The Indispensable Guide to Practically Everything:
Jesus

The Indispensable Guide to Practically Everything:
Life After Death & Heaven and Hell

The Indispensable Guide to Practically Everything:
Prayer

The Indispensable Guide to Practically Everything:
World Religions and What People Believe